LEARNING PHONICS AND SPELLING

in a Whole Language Classroom

by
Debbie Powell
Associate Professor, Reading
University of Northern Colorado
Greeley, Colorado

and
David Hornsby
Principal, Ringwood Heights Primary School
Melbourne, Australia

SCHOLASTIC
PROFESSIONAL BOOKS

New York • Tornoto • London • Auckland • Sydney

ACKNOWLEDGMENTS

e thank the many teachers who regularly shared their classrooms and students' work with us. We learned so much from each of these professionals and recognize that our writing would have no credibility without them. Specifically, we would like to thank Gayle Baker, Helen Farthing, Zena Goodman, Cheryl Grambau, Cathy Lasell, Mary McDonald, Marilyn Perry, Jean Rachubinski, Elaine Viscek, and Nadine Watson. We would also like to thank all of the children for sharing their work and personal stories with us.

We also thank our families for their patience and support. Finally, we would like to thank Terry Cooper for having faith in our ideas and in us as writers.

The illustrated version of "Peter Peter Pumpkin Eater," from *Three Bags Full*, (Rigby Education, Chicago) is reproduced by permission of Mimosa Publications, 8 Yarra Street, Hawthorn, 3122, Australia.

Design by Nancy Metcalf

Production by Intergraphics

Cover design by Vincent Ceci and Drew Hires

Illustrations by Teresa Anderko

ISBN 0-590-49148-2

CONTENTS

continued

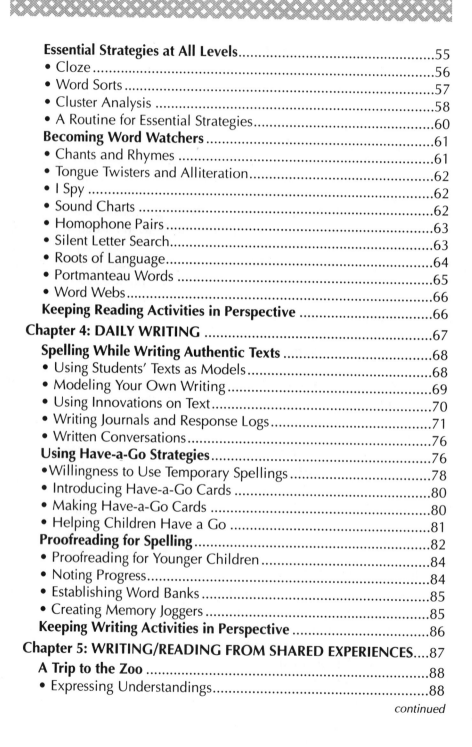

continued

continued

The Essentials

Despite the continuing debate which places phonics/spelling and whole language at opposite ends of a mythical continuum, there is general agreement that children still need to learn graphophonic connections. This book will explore some of the ways that whole language teachers can help their students make these connections.

Because many emerging and novice whole language teachers today are somewhat confused about the role of spelling and phonics in the whole language philosophy, this first section will help to clarify how phonics and spelling are essential elements in the entire curriculum.

The goal of this book, in fact, is to give support to all teachers who are questioning their beliefs and who are engaging in learning themselves. This section and the remainder of this book, therefore, offer you models and possibilities to explore in order to keep your beliefs about learning, language, curriculum, and teaching consistent.

Chapter 1

Phonics and Spelling in Perspective

> This book is to help you—the emerging, novice, or experienced whole language teacher—consider or clarify the place of phonics and spelling in your meaning-centered program.

From the very first day of school at every grade level, whole language teachers begin with real reading and writing experiences that focus on meaning because they want their students to quickly learn that reading and writing are for communication. As children are learning to read and write, they are also learning phonics and spelling. Phonics, after all, is an integral part of comprehending, and spelling is an integral part of writing. However, the issues are: 1) how children learn graphophonic relationships; 2) when they learn them, and; 3) what the appropriate contexts are. The extreme positions taken by some educators have set up false dichotomies that we believe just don't exist in practice. For example, we don't accept the notion that whole language teachers have caused a deficit in children's reading skills due to a lack of phonics instruction. On the other hand, we do believe that whole language teachers need to teach phonics and spelling—but in meaningful contexts.

Learning Phonics and Spelling

Within the context of reading and writing, whole language teachers can, in fact, help most children learn letter-sound correspondence and spelling patterns with little or no direct instruction. This doesn't mean that they don't teach these connections; they do, and most use strategies like the following examples.

• Modeling the actual processes of reading and writing.
• Immersing children in these processes even though their attempts may be primitive approximations for writing and reading.
• Subtly drawing attention to letters, their sounds, and spelling patterns always in the context of reading and writing.
• Occasionally and more directly focusing on letter-sound relationships and spelling patterns though still within a context that recognizes the integration of all cueing systems and the overriding importance of meaning.

Three Cueing Systems

Almost all young children make the transition from scribbles to conventional writing and from babbling while turning pages in a book to "real" reading. How do they do this? This transformation occurs as they develop their abilities to use semantic, syntactic, and graphophonic cues.

In other words, children are able to process language when they can use graphophonic cues (letters, letter clusters, and often their corresponding sounds) along with semantic (meaning) and syntactic (grammar) cues interactively and almost simultaneously while reading and writing. They integrate these three cues with their own background knowledge and the broader situational and social context to *decode* and *encode* messages in text. Perhaps the following example will clarify this concept.

What word would you predict for the unknown word in this sentence? (The word is printed, but you don't recognize it.)

They_____across the road.

Responses are numerous and usually include such words as *walked, ran, darted, rolled, skidded, slid, jumped, flew,* and so on. Without thinking consciously about parts of speech and tenses, knowledgeable respondents always give a verb in either past tense or present tense. You know the word cannot be a noun or another part of speech, and you also know the verb cannot be in the future tense. (People generally operate subconsciously on this knowledge of how language works.) Knowledge about the structure and patterns of language is often referred to as *syntactic knowledge.* If you predicted a verb in the past or present tense, you are an effective reader. However, in this particular instance, your goal is to read exactly what the word is. (Remember that the word is there, but it is an unknown word.) To decode the word, therefore, you'll need more information—perhaps the preceding sentence.

David dropped his tennis balls.
They_____across the road.

What would you predict for the unknown word now? *rolled? bounced?*

The extra sentence gives additional cues about meaning that come from your knowledge of the subject. (You know about tennis balls and what they do when they have been dropped.) You now have fewer choices because you are constrained by this *semantic knowledge.*

You now can confidently narrow your choice down to just two words, but that is not good enough. You want to know exactly what the unknown word is. Therefore, you still need further information —perhaps the first letter of the unknown word.

continued

> **David dropped his tennis balls.**
>
> **They *r*_____ across the road.**
>
> It is almost certain now that you will predict that the word is *rolled*, even if you had never seen it in print before. A beginning reader, of course, might need to be reminded of known words that start with *r* —words, for example, that might have been accumulating on a class chart during a week of working with "Little Red Riding Hood." Knowledge of the relationships between sounds and letters and of the way words look is called *graphophonic knowledge*.

From the time children begin to develop language, they use semantic and syntactic cues to create meaning. This fact does not, however, exclude or diminish the importance of graphophonic cues. After readers, for example, make predictions based on meaning and grammatical cues, they are able to check their predictions by referring to letters or letter clusters—primarily those at the beginning of words. In the example above, you needed graphophonic knowledge to determine that the word was *rolled* rather than *bounced*.

Also keep in mind that letter-sound relationships and spelling patterns are even more important for writing than they are for reading. Most children will learn to use graphophonic cues by modeling proficient readers and writers and by reading and writing in a variety of contexts. Their very early attempts are often obvious approximations of the processes, but these sustain the learners' needs, nevertheless, and provide purpose for learning phonics and spelling.

The Need for Graphophonic Instruction

All children have a need to learn graphophonic relationships, but only some need really specific instruction in phonics and spelling. However, many teachers feel that they need to teach phonics and spelling to all children because of the political climate in which they teach and/or because of eventual accountability. Nevertheless, we believe that the activities inherent in whole language reading and writing experiences—activities such as repeated readings, finger pointing, framing of spelling patterns, finding rhyming words, finding words that start with the same letter or letter cluster—all naturally support the learning of phonics and spelling. More importantly, when your curriculum focuses on meaning-making and when authentic texts are used, many children will actually want to engage in the problem-solving involved in reading and writing. These same children usually take more responsibility for their learning, in general, and tackle graphophonic learning within this broader picture.

For most children, this natural coverage of graphophonic cues is enough. However, when a child's oral reading miscues, or variations from text, and temporary spellings indicate a lack of graphophonic knowledge, you can provide additional help with little intrusion. (*In Section II, you will read about strategies that will make the learning of phonics and spelling easier than what is normally assumed, and in Chapters 2 and 6 you will learn how to identify those children who need more focus on phonics and spelling.*)

Try not to lose sight of the fact that all three types of cues help children construct meaning. To put too much emphasis on graphophonics, for example, may create word-callers rather than readers and writers. When children aren't making graphophonic connections, they need to strengthen their use of the other two cueing systems while they learn at least beginning and ending consonant sounds. Also keep in mind that some students may not learn to distinguish vowel sounds that are taught in isolation, but these same children can still learn to decode effectively when they use all three cueing systems. These same children can also learn to spell if their sight and meaning strategies are strengthened while they are learning letter-sound relationships.

The Use of Authentic Texts

Choose reading materials that your students can really sink their teeth into—materials that will put another world inside their heads. And if you want them to continue to read, the materials should engage their imaginations and stir their emotions so that they will laugh, feel sad, and/or sit in wonder. The texts should also extend their knowledge and leave them asking for more.

The materials you use in your classroom will likely influence your students' attitudes towards reading and writing. What "readers read makes all the difference to their view of reading" (Meek, 1981). Similarly, we also believe that what readers read makes all the difference to their view of writing.

The goal of your students' writing should be to write engaging texts. You can't expect good writing—the kind that truly captivates the reader—unless your students are exposed to authentic text models. Such texts would obviously include both fiction and nonfiction literature, as well as songs, recipes, and your students' personal writing.

While your students are reading and writing meaningful and interesting texts, you can help them focus on phonic and spelling elements. For example, when sharing these texts with children, you can highlight a particular graphophonic element—whether it be an initial letter, a final letter, a letter cluster, or a common ending. *The texts you use generally dictate the phonics and spelling your students will learn—rather than the other way around.* This means that whole language teachers must use a wide variety of authentic texts in their classrooms to assure that all graphophonic elements will be learned.

Although graphophonic relationships are often taught spontaneously, you should also plan ahead. For example, when using *The Three Billy-Goats Gruff* with your class, instinctively you would probably highlight *tr* as in "troll" and "Trip, trap! Trip, trap!"

However, when your students' work shows that a particular graphophonic relationship such as *tr* needs emphasis, then it is quite legitimate for you to select literature that has a high incidence of the *tr* cluster so you can emphasize that skill. Such planned teaching can still be unobtrusive and natural.

Principles for Skills Learning in General

You can use the following general principles as a guide when helping your students learn reading and writing skills.

1. **Your students should develop as independent learners.** As they learn skills, they will rely less and less on you and others. In other words, they will become more confident in their own abilities to "have a go" and to become explorers of language.

2. **Your students should see the relevancy of a skill for themselves.** Most children, for example, will voluntarily engage in learning sound-symbol relationships when they have a need for them in reading and writing.

3. **Your time should be used effectively.** Although it is sometimes appropriate to spend a few minutes helping one or two children learn a particular skill, it is generally more effective to plan small-group work based on the information your students have gained from cooperative reading, writing, listening, and observing. Children naturally learn skills while they are learning content and while they are practicing other aspects of the bigger processes of reading and writing. You'll probably find that once children know particular skills, they will do some of the teaching for you—and do it quite effectively.

4. **Normally you should use inquiry or inductive strategies rather than direct teaching strategies, but at certain times both may be appropriate.** Inquiry strategies encourage children to consider various examples and then to reason and develop generalizations. For example, after children have listed words containing the letter *c* (such as *cent, cat, city, coat, cut,* and *nice*),

15

you can help them form the generalization about the soft and hard sounds of the letter *c*. Occasionally, however, you may find it appropriate to teach deductively. In other words, you may want to provide a generalization and then have your students find examples.

5. **You should demonstrate skills in action.** The most effective skills teaching occurs during purposeful writing and reading events when you demonstrate the skills in action. You may use strategies such as the following.

   • Modelled writing.

   • Shared writing of wall stories.

   • Shared reading using a big book or chart.

   • Dramatic reading for a group performance.

Principles for Learning Graphophonic Skills in Particular

Our philosophy and strategies for teaching phonics and spelling are based on the following three premises.

1. **Have your students learn graphophonic relationships in context.** Because letter-sound relationships are artificial and distorted when taught in isolation, you should teach graphophonics skills in context by capitalizing on the oral language being generated in the room, on the texts being written, and on the texts available from other sources. Then during the actual processes of reading or writing, draw attention to spelling patterns and letter-sound relationships as learning needs dictate. As much as possible, therefore, your students should solve graphophonic problems *themselves*, although some prompting, such as the following, may be appropriate.

Reading

   • What word do you think would make sense there?

   • How did you know that word?

Spelling

- What sounds do you hear in the word?
- How would you spell that word?

You and your students should also play with words—including such activities as reciting tongue twisters, noting rhyming words, and playing I Spy. In this way, they will learn graphophonics skills in context—in situations that are meaningful and purposeful.

2. **Teach letter-sound relationships as only one way of dealing with written language.** Graphophonic cues comprise only one of the cueing systems available for help in reconstructing an author's message. Young readers must also learn how to use their knowledge of language structure and grammar (syntactic cues) and their world and experiential knowledge (semantic cues) for decoding.

3. **Be cautious that you do not take away your students' need for graphophonic skills.** When children are writing for themselves and using temporary spellings, they quickly realize how important it is to learn sound-symbol relationships. However, when teachers write for them or spell words for them, they will often stop sounding out words and lose their need for graphophonic knowledge.

   Similarly, when children are reading and are unable to recognize words, you should not always provide the words. Rather, use such opportunities to help them learn word-recognition strategies. For example, instead of asking a student to "sound it out," encourage her to read the text before and after the unknown word to see if context (syntactic and semantic) cues help. She should look at the first letter (or letter cluster) of the word and, relying on sound-symbol relationships, be able to make a prediction. (Context cues plus graphophonic cues provide powerful assistance for recognition of unknown words.)

   If you supply the unknown words too readily, your students may fail to realize the *need* for graphophonic knowledge. Most teachers quickly learn how to shift from reading for and with students (shared reading) to allowing them to take risks and read for themselves (guided reading and independent reading). You will also learn when to supply words and when to encourage your students to utilize strategies to decode for themselves.

Methods Carry Messages

The methods you use carry messages to your students and help to shape their definitions of reading and writing. Therefore, you will want to send the following messages so that students will become lifelong readers and writers: 1) reading and writing are supposed to make sense; 2) reading and writing are useful tools for learning and solving problems; and 3) reading, writing, and the quest for knowledge can be enjoyable. As a whole language teacher, you need to employ methods that not only model proficient reading and writing but that also economize effort and scaffold learning in such a way as to prevent useless wanderings. Rather than leaving phonics and spelling development to chance, look for opportunities to systematically draw attention to the alphabet, to rhyming patterns, to spelling patterns, and to letter-sound relationships in the context of quality literature and other authentic texts—without overemphasizing these aspects of reading and writing. A good test is to ask yourself, "Why am I using these materials in this way?" Your answer should always include the value of the literary content as well as the skills that can be highlighted.

Graphophonics and Reading

Over the years, phonics has been referred to as 1) a method of teaching reading; 2) instructional activities to teach reading; and even 3) instructional activities that emphasize sound-symbol correspondence. There have also been frequent references to phonic analysis (the identification of words by their sounds) and to phonic generalizations (the rules indicating under which conditions a letter or group of letters represents a particular sound). (Harris & Hodges,

1981) Because terminology has been anything but clear, there sometimes has been a misunderstanding that phonics and whole language are at opposite ends of a mythical continuum. Although we are not advocating an eclectic view, we do believe that teachers can help children learn graphophonic relationships through a whole language philosophy.

We chose to use the terms *phonics* and *spelling* because they are common terms, but in this book, we defined *phonics* as "letter-sound correspondences." Still, we are also referring to the general graphophonic knowledge that readers use as they read (and write) because we think that that is how most teachers define *phonics*. In fact, we find that most teachers view phonics in the broad sense as spelling patterns, rhyming words, matching initial sounds, letter recognition, and so on, and specifically as letter-sound correspondences. There is not a simple one-to-one correspondence between sound and symbol. These sound-symbol correspondences vary from word to word or from speaker to speaker because of different spelling patterns, dialect differences, and individual pronunciations. (We found this is especially true as we—an Aussie and an American—were writing this book together.) On the other hand, there is a regularity and logic to the English language that young children pick up independently of any instruction. For instance, most two- and three-year-olds are able to generalize that the -*ed* suffix means past tense, and they regularly add -*ed* to words even when they have never heard such words spoken: *goed, runned,* and *comed.* (Of course, it usually doesn't take long for children to learn the exceptions to these generalizations.) Young children's regular use of rhyme and alliteration illustrates their ability to form generalizations about initial sounds and rhyming patterns.

It is this general graphophonic knowledge that we want you to think about when we refer to *phonics*—as opposed to mere individual letter-sound relationships.

Phonics for Confirming Predictions

Although there is conflicting evidence as to the role of graphophonic cues in reading (Adams, 1990; Goswami & Bryant, 1990; Weaver, 1988, 1990; Smith, 1982), what is clear is that spelling patterns—rather than specific letter-sound correspondences—are important to the reading process. It is also apparent that the better the match between the reader's background knowledge and the context (semantic or syntactic cues), the less attention the reader needs to give to graphophonic cues. Proficient readers will use graphophonic knowledge to confirm or reject their predictions; not every letter or letter cluster is of equal usefulness. The graphophonic cues at the beginning of words, for example, are generally the most helpful. Therefore, the use of confirming and rejecting strategies is apparent when readers read a word or phrase aloud and go back and self-correct what they have read. Use of these strategies may also be detected in retellings when readers correct a word or phrase that they mispronounced when reading orally.

Using Confirming Strategies

When 8-year-old Matthew was reading a newspaper article about his favorite baseball player, he read *baseball* when the text said *basketball*. He had expected the word to be *baseball* because he associated the player with that sport. However, that section of the article was describing the player's attempt at playing basketball. When Matthew suddenly realized that the game being described was actually basketball, he immediately went back to the first use of the word, noted that there was a *k* /c/ in it, and commented on his failure to have noticed it previously. For him, the *k* confirmed (in addition to the context) that the word was *basketball* rather than *baseball*.

Decoding: One Strategy in Comprehending

Decoding is another reading term with multiple meanings and connotations. Most teachers define *decoding* as "sounding out a word" or "using letter-sound correspondences to unlock the pronunciation of a word." To us, *decoding* means "the entire set of strategies readers use when they investigate, or unlock, words." This equates *decoding* in reading to *spelling* in writing. In other words, *decoding* is the use of all available graphophonic, syntactic, and semantic cues when processing words during reading. It shouldn't be hard to see, therefore, how our definition of *decoding* encompasses much more than just the sounding out of words. It also involves the unique set of strategies that readers may become most conscious of using when they come to words they don't know.

Keep in mind, as well, that decoding is just one small part of comprehending. Proficient readers easily recognize most words and gain meaning usually without even attending to all of the letters or even all of the words, because their ability to decode is largely automatic and subconscious. However, when these same readers come to words they don't immediately recognize, they employ a series of strategies that are reader-specific. In other words, there is not just one effective decoding strategy.

The decoding strategies readers use depend on their purpose for reading. For instance, if a reader picks up a novel to read purely for pleasure, the first decoding strategy he or she uses for unknown words may be to skim over them. On the other hand, if the same reader is going to be responsible for rereading a passage aloud, he or she will probably use a decoding strategy that involves looking up words in the dictionary and studying their correct pronunciations. When spelling a word, a student employs a series of visual, phonic, semantic, and syntactic strategies to write the word correctly, and that same student employs a series of decoding strategies to investigate an unknown word when reading. For example, a child may use the following set of decoding strategies when reading—and wanting to understand—a nonfiction book about birds.

Decoding

1. As the student skims the information in the book, she automatically decodes most words because she has read other books about birds.

2. When she comes to an unknown word, she keeps reading, although she is conscious that she doesn't recognize the word. After several more paragraphs, she realizes that the text isn't making sense. She then backs up and rereads the paragraph containing the unknown word. As she does, she uses all of the semantic, syntactic, and graphophonic cues.

3. This time, the deep structure, or meaning, of the sentence helps her get the gist of the word. This general meaning seems enough because she can now understand the remaining text. She doesn't need to confirm what the exact word is.

The illustration above is just one example and would not, of course, be the decoding strategies that the same reader would use when reading different material for a different purpose.

Always keep in mind, therefore, that phonics is a part of graphophonic knowledge; graphophonic cues are part of decoding strategies; and decoding is a small part of comprehending. You must keep all of this in perspective.

Graphophonics and Writing

You can monitor your students' development in spelling by observing the challenges that they face and what they do to meet those challenges. For example, one of the earliest challenges all young writers face is what to write about. A concurrent challenge is spelling—getting down on paper the conventional symbols used for representing sounds. In fact, young writers generally find spelling the dominant challenge, and they often change spellings before attending to any other tasks involved in the process of writing (Graves, 1983;

Calkins, 1986). Sometimes they will even change their meaning in order to spell words correctly. In the past, most teachers separated spelling instruction from writing; now, whole language teachers include spelling as a part of writing. However, some whole language teachers have said they lack confidence to evaluate spelling needs and to intervene at the point of need. They have accepted approximations in temporary spellings but haven't understood how to interpret them. For example, a child who writes *fesh* for *fish* knows that the word has a vowel but may not be able to hear the difference between a short *e* and a short *i*. (This is common with children under 6 or 7.) A child who writes *chrain* for *train* is actually writing what he or she hears. A child who writes *wg* for *dog* has reasoned that the initial sound *d* is represented by the letter *w* (say the name of the letter *w* out loud and listen to the first sound). The more you understand what the nature of spelling development is and how to support that development throughout the curriculum, the less you will have to worry about it.

Spelling Development

Although several researchers have described developmental stages of spelling (Henderson & Beers, 1980; Gentry, 1982), we feel that there are no stages of development in terms of the strategies spellers use because the strategies beginning spellers use are the same as those of mature spellers. What varies is their experience and background knowledge (Harste, Woodward and Burke, 1984). In fact, we think that the simpler the categorization of development, the better—especially since children may very well display a wide variety of spelling behaviors that cross the following three phases.

23

EMERGENT SPELLERS

Emergent spellers understand the function of print. They begin to use print to communicate meaning, but they don't have sufficient graphophonic knowledge to communicate a message through writing alone because they use predominantly temporary spellings.

Observations:

- uses letter—like symbols
- no indication that child has:
  1. letter knowledge
  2. letter/sound correspondences
  3. sense of wordness
- has idea that print carries message

Three Billy Goats Gruff, but there are six.

Observations:

- uses both initial and final sounds of words
- several conventional spellings
- capitalized *I* in second use
- uses dash to indicate letters missing
- uses some vowels
- word segmentation not evident

I was at the school today and I went to the gym today.

NOVICE SPELLERS

Novice spellers have enough graphophonic knowledge to communicate meaning to others, but they use temporary spelling when writing unknown words and sometimes even when writing words they have frequently written before. They predominantly use phonic strategies for spelling.

Observations:

- word segmentation
- may need assistance with placement on page
- uses vowels consistently
- uncertainty of some spelling patterns (such as *sh*)
- uses primarily uppercase letters

RYAN

A GOST is A BAD SPERIT YOU CAN FID HEM iN A HtEDHAOZ SO You HOD NOt Go iN tO it

Observations:

- most sounds represented with reasonable letter/sounds
- many conventionally spelled words
- word segmentation used
- spacing on page may need attention
- mixes lowercase and uppercase
- vowels used consistently in each syllable

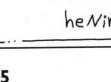

A Bird A storey iSABird wusApoNAtiM thAr wus ALitL Bird And he did Not NoWA to go Sohe CApt oN woc iNg he Nir stopt And

INDEPENDENT SPELLERS

Independent spellers use conventional spelling for most words frequently written, and they have developed efficient strategies for spelling unknown words. They have also developed proofreading strategies.

Observations:

- mostly correct spelling
- knows hyphenated vowels and contractions
- mixes lower- and uppercase letters
- uses letter format
- needs attention on punctuation and capitals

> Dear Scott
> I ho pe you get to Be A Teacher HiS iS my FirST Time To Be A pen-Pal And iS FУn Being youer peh-Pal. if you AreMy Teacher Thenyou'lBe AS good AS Any. OTher TeACher. IhAve to puppies do you have Any PeTS
>
> from you'en pen-PAl
>
> DAVid

Observations:

- mostly correct spelling
- knows hyphenated words, compound words
- spells plural forms
- proofreading skills not apparent

> Dress-Up
> I like to dress up with Jennifer. We put onfancy dresses and gloves and very pretty Purses. We put on high hill shoes. And We put on Make up. And we like to play house with the dresses. Some day Iwith that I can wear every thing in Public, but I dought it.
>
> The End

It is important to remember that any developmental phases or stages, no matter how they are described, are continuous and overlapping, and children will vary widely in their development within and across these phases. As a result, you need to look for *clusters of behaviors* when you describe spelling progress.

Three Major Spelling Strategies

The use of graphophonic knowledge constitutes only one of the major spelling strategies. The other two are visual memory and morphemic knowledge. We've included a brief discussion of these two to help you become aware of the different ways you can help your students with them.

To begin, consider the following three lists of words.

Group 1	Group 2	Group 3
Ayatollah	asclepiadaceous	dissatisfied
fuchsia	coloxolyn	disapprove
diarrhea	syzygy	unnecessary
vignette	Mymidon	Mediterranean

If these words were dictated to you, how would you spell them? The following responses are typical among teachers and parents.

Group 1: "Oh, no! I knew you would give me words like that. I just read the word *Ayatollah* in the paper the other day, but I know I won't be able to spell it." *(Adults usually will then write the word to see if it looks correct.)*

Group 2: "What did you say? Please say it again... slowly. Can you use the word in a sentence? What does it mean?"

Group 3: *"Dissatisfied.* Now does that have one or two *s*'s? Hmm, *Mediterranean.* Is that one or two *t*'s and one or two *r*'s?"

If you ask adults to spell words like those in the first group, their common response is one of knowing the word and what it means, but also realizing that they are going to have trouble spelling it. Usually they are not only familiar with the word, but they also can use it as part of their oral vocabulary. Although they know that "sounding out" the word won't help them, they often feel that if they write the word how they think it may be spelled, they will be able to judge whether it's correct or not by looking at it. They are, therefore, relying on their *visual memory.*

If you ask the same adults to spell the words in the second group, their responses are usually immediate. They probably would not use these words in their own speech, and often they have no idea what the words mean—even if they have heard them before. Since they can't visualize the words, they know that the only way they can attempt to spell them is by listening carefully and then trying to represent the sounds they hear with printed symbols. In other words, they have to rely on their knowledge of *graphophonic relationships.*

Finally, if you asked the same adults to spell the words in the third group, they usually show less concern than they did with the words in the second group because the words are familiar. Still, sometimes they reveal their uncertainties in spelling these words by considering the units of meaning called *morphemes.* A *morpheme* is "the smallest unit of meaning in written language, and it involves both semantic and syntactic information." For example, some people know how to spell *Mediterranean* because they know that the parts of the word mean "in the middle/the land/the sea." When they also know that *terra* means "land," they will be able to spell *Mediterranean* with the right number of *t*'s and *r*'s. When spellers solve spelling problems by using information they know about words and word parts, they are using *morphemic knowledge.*

Even very young children have a great deal of morphemic knowledge. For example, in their first year at school—if they *speak* the language—they already know different forms of the same word such as:

jump/jumps/jumping/jumped
happy/unhappy

To review, the three major spelling strategies that adults and children use are based on the following.

- **Visual memory** of spelling patterns. Writers get a picture of a word in their head.
- **Graphophonic or sound-symbol knowledge**. Writers listen to the sounds in words and then write down letters for those sounds.
- **Morphemic or word knowledge**. Young writers use what they know about some words to help them spell other words.

Keep in mind that students can develop all three of these spelling strategies as they read and write authentic texts, but they will need you to demonstrate these strategies and to orchestrate teaching situations and procedures that will direct their attention to spelling-strategy development.

Chapter 2

The Whole Picture

> In a broad sense, you could say that the content of your curriculum is "life's experiences."

There are few life experiences that cannot be accounted for under the broad headings science and social studies. What does this have to do with learning phonics and spelling? We think everything! The integrated curriculum, combining science and social studies with language, mathematics, and the arts, is the heart of the whole language curriculum.

Phonics and Spelling in the Whole Curriculum

Traditionally, elementary teachers considered science and social studies as subjects that were "nice for students to know" if they had time to teach them. However, in an integrated curriculum, the exploration and understanding of the social and physical sciences give children a purpose—a personal reason—for engaging in reading and

writing authentic text. As a result, they will have a need for the conventions of phonics and spelling. (See Pidgon & Woolley, 1992, for a more detailed explanation of integrated curriculum.)

For the purpose of this book it is important that you keep conventions, such as phonics and spelling, in perspective within the larger curriculum picture. When you consider reading and writing as ways of exploring and expressing life experiences, phonics and spelling, and even reading and writing, should be considered as *means* and not *ends* in the whole language, integrated curriculum.

Finding Time for an Integrated Curriculum

It is only through *sustained interactions* with text (including composing it and comprehending it) and multiple opportunities to interact with others in all language modes that children will have the contact with language to develop the skills, strategies, understandings, and attitudes that are necessary for literacy.

However, whole language teachers are realizing that the time they spend on literacy in the content areas is every bit as important as the time they spend during language arts. After all, the life-literacy we hope to develop involves much more than the reading and writing of stories that has dominated in language arts. Consider the possibilities for reading and writing throughout the day, and you will see all of these possibilities as opportunities for children to learn and apply literacy skills and strategies. As teachers "think literacy," they find opportunities to teach skills in context, whether that context is language arts, science, or social studies.

When children are engaged with interesting content they *generate* language—both oral and written. This language is not "frills on the edge of the program;" it can be the *core* of the program when the teacher knows how to harness it.

An Integrated Curriculum

A group of students in a third-grade classroom described to their teacher how they made a wormery. Afterwards they wrote "how-to-do-it" instructions for the rest of the class. Once they had completed their first draft, they revised it for meaning, and then their teacher taught them the various language features that are common to a procedural text—such as chronological linking words (*first, last, then, later*); present tense action verbs (*mix, pour, place, grip*); and detailed descriptions of the materials (*amount, color, texture, type, density*). This science activity, therefore, was a vehicle for significant language learning. (*Chapter 5 will provide an extended example of how language teaching and learning can be based on shared experiences from other content areas.*)

When language is used in an integrated curriculum, the children with the greatest needs—those who have failed to see the need for phonics and spelling or those who are having difficulty learning graphophonic connections—often gain the most because the content is more likely to engage their interest and, thereby, motivate them. It is very likely, for example, that such students would learn effortlessly about the *w* /w/ relationship when writing about the worms in the wormery.

We don't believe that children naturally learn all phonics and spelling skills (or any other skills for that matter) by engaging with content only. We believe that teachers thoughtfully orchestrate opportunities for skills learning while children are reading and writing about content that is significant to them. This requires you to think about what is important for children to learn about literacy. What do particular students need to know? Which teaching techniques can best facilitate this instruction within the context of reading and writing? And what possibilities do the available texts (such as fiction, nonfiction, children's own writing, and the teacher's writing) provide for particular skill instruction?

Developing a Timetable

The kinds of connections made in the example of the wormery can actually be maintained throughout an entire day. The following timetable shows one way in which you might organize a typical school day—following an integrated curriculum. The timetable also shows the varying roles you and your students might play at different times.

SCLASSROOM
napshot

Sample Daily Timetable

TEACHER

Focus: Language Arts

9:00 Focus on helping your students with READING skills and strategies (including phonics), understandings, behaviors, and attitudes.

10:00 Focus on helping your students with WRITING skills and strategies (including spelling), understandings, behaviors, and attitudes.

11:00 Morning Recess

Focus: Math

11:20 Focus on helping your students with math skills, strategies, understandings, behaviors, and attitudes.

CHILDREN

Focus: Learning

Children are READING self-selected materials, texts related to the integrated unit, texts related to their own inquiries, and/or WRITING their own texts related to the integrated unit being studied. Their activities may also include dramatic and artistic expression.

Focus: Learning

Children are involved in inquiry to math learning and/or math related to or generated by the integrated

continued

33

unit. Children are applying reading/writing skills and strategies (including phonics and spelling) for learning math. Their activities may also include dramatic and artistic expression.

12:20 Lunch

Focus: Investigation—
Communication

Focus: Learning

Integrated Unit: (Content from social studies, science, and health)

1:20 Focus on helping your students with the inquiry process and with the development of concepts and generalizations related to social studies, science, health, and any other content areas in the curriculum.

Children are involved in inquiry, including:
• tuning-in activities;
• collecting and sorting data;
• presenting and science, health, reporting data; and
• application (reporting, social action, and so on). Includes reading/writing related to the content and inquiry (and application of phonics and spelling). Their activities may also include dramatic, musical, and artistic expression.

3:30 Dismissal

Adapted from Hornsby et.al., 1992.

When you are able to capitalize on natural learning links that exist among areas of curriculum, your students will be reading and writing virtually all day—every day—and not just during language arts sessions (Hornsby & Parry, 1992; Pappas, C. et. al., 1990; Routman R., 1991). Although there is likely still a need for reading, writing, and math workshops, your role during workshop time will be to help facilitate the learning of *process*.

Between 10:00 and 11:00, for example, a group of students may be writing newspaper articles for the class newspaper based on an integrated unit on weather. Of course, they know that they can receive assistance with any writing because that is your focus at that time. However, if their need is for more facts or for clarification of some meteorological concept, they would know that it is up to them to independently find this information or that they should wait for your assistance during the afternoon when you will be focusing on content. Often it is your students who will carry over the theme and understandings from the content area to your reading, writing, or math workshops, though you may also choose to do so. Other times the reading, writing, and math will be unrelated to the unit of study.

The Importance of Routines

Many who have done research in whole language classrooms—including Calkins (1983, 1986), Graves (1983, 1984), and Hansen (1987)—have written about the importance of structure and routines in the classroom. Likewise, many practicing teachers have done the same (Atwell, 1987; Fisher, 1991; Parry & Hornsby, 1988; Routman, 1991). All of these educators agree that a whole language classroom needs to be highly structured so that both the teacher and the children will have very definite routines to follow. Jane Hansen says that whole language teachers usually develop an "inner structure" that often remains undetected from other teachers who are looking for the familiar "exostructure" (1987). Nevertheless, the structure is there, and it is often deceptively simple. Whole language teachers often spend a considerable amount of time at the beginning of the school year establishing the desired structure with their children and, they always negotiate change as needed throughout the year.

Routines Encourage Independence

Whole language teachers recognize the importance of their students' taking some responsibility for their own learning by making decisions about their work. And once these students know how their classroom operates, most will learn to work independently and cooperatively on research, writing, and other projects without their teacher's direct guidance. With routines, children can engage in meaningful and often long-term projects that require them to learn skills and strategies as well as significant content learning. Students also know what to expect from their teacher and when to expect it. In the following paragraph, Calkins reinforces the need for structure.

"It is significant to realize the most creative environments in our society are not the ever-changing ones. The artist's studio, the researcher's laboratory, and the scholar's library are each deliberately kept simple so as to support the complexities of the work-in-progress. They are deliberately kept predictable, so the unpredictable can happen." (1983, p. 32)

The structure you establish in your classroom will allow routines to develop. Then, by following your routines religiously, by modeling appropriate forms of response, and by reinforcing appropriate forms of response, you will be able to expect work habits to develop more quickly because your classroom will become more predictable. Rather than filling every minute of your school day with activities, you will be able to allot time everyday for workshops—time for your students to read and write independently and with others in cooperative groups. What's more, you will be able to *expect* your students to know what to do next and how to work by themselves and with others—without directions and constant supervison. Not only should you have a predictable routine for reading-writing workshops, but you also should develop routines for learning and practicing particular skills and strategies during your workshops. For example, the routine for how and when your students attend to spelling should be as predictable as is the time to write in your classroom. In the following example, you will see how David used a particular routine he developed for teaching spelling with a multi-age class, including grades 2, 3, and 4. Since all students followed the same routine, David was able to address his students' individual differences while still making sure each child felt a part of the community of learners. Although you will want to adapt this routine to meet your own needs, remember that the object is to establish routines for reading-writing workshops—as well as routines for teaching/learning particular skills.

Spelling Routines

1. **Write.** Since David had his students write every day, they had daily needs to spell. David worked hard to develop attitudes and writing behaviors in his students that promoted writing and that gave them confidence. To accomplish these goals, he often modeled, reinforced, and encouraged his students to operate with a "have-a-go spirit" as they wrote down their ideas. This have-a-go spirit prepared them to use temporary spellings, temporarily!

2. **Proofread.** After his students drafted and revised their ideas, David often expected them to proofread their work. Because he required conventional spelling if the writers were going to publish their works for others to read, he used some of the activities described in Chapter 4 to teach proofreading skills during small-group or whole-class mini-lessons. He usually started with children underlining words they felt needed attention. (See pages 82-84.)

3. **Negotiate.** After his students proofread their work and underlined any words needing attention, David sat down with each child and negotiated how many of the underlined words needed to be

continued

Snapshot *continued*

attended to. He based his decisions on the confidence and capability of the individual students. For example, he required confident, capable spellers to correct all or most of the underlined words, but less confident spellers had to address only three or four of the underlined words. Then he had his students use a variety of strategies—including the next step—to correct their misspelled words.

4. **Use Have-A-Go Cards.** David told his students to copy the required number of underlined words from their writing to a have-a-go card, like the one below. After students tried alternative spellings, David, a parent helper, or a cross-age tutor provided assistance if necessary. Eventually he used the third column of the card to write the words correctly, even if the students had spelled them correctly themselves during one of their attempts. (Have-a-go cards are explained in further detail in Chapter 4, including strategies teachers can use when helping their students arrive at correct spellings. See pages 80-82).

Directions: Cut the third column off to make your personal spelling list.

HAVE-A-GO CARD		TEACHER or helper writes correct words in this column	This personal list belongs to:
How I spelled the word in my writing	Have-A-Go		

continued

In addition to the use of have-a-go cards, other strategies for correcting misspelled words include having students check for spellings of words on wall charts; having them refer to sound charts like the ones on pages 148-152 in the Appendix; or having them ask a friend, check in familiar books, and/or use a dictionary.

5. **Develop Personal Spelling Lists.** Then David showed his students how to use the final column on their have-a-go cards as a personal spelling list, and he taught them to practice the words on their personal lists with the look/cover/write/check procedure. He also showed them how to cut up the third (teacher) column of their personal spelling lists into word cards for practicing the words in various activities. When various students were ready to be tested on the words on their personal spelling lists, they notified David by placing their lists on his clipboard.

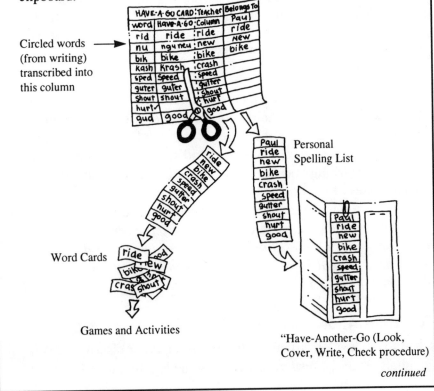

Circled words (from writing) transcribed into this column

Personal Spelling List

Word Cards

Games and Activities

"Have-Another-Go (Look, Cover, Write, Check procedure)

continued

Snapshot *continued*

David usually checked his students' spelling whenever he had a few free minutes rather than at scheduled times, and it took him only about one minute per child to give and check the words. Afterwards he monitored his students' progress and the regularity with which they came forward for testing. David found that his students learned more words this way than they ever did with weekly spelling tests. Finally, he kept the personal spelling lists in a file, and he showed them to parents during parent/teacher conferences.

6. **Publish.** When student writers in David's class went to publish their work, they first consulted with the editorial committee (David plus a few students who were rotated monthly). The committee members asked each writer, "Why do you want to publish this piece of writing?" A writer usually answered by referring to his or her process, growth, strengths, and so on. Once the final decision was made to publish, David sat down with the student and functioned the way a real-life editor does. He helped the student correct any remaining misspellings, and he addressed other writing conventions like punctuation and capitalization.

It's important to point out here that a routine such as the one just described does not, and should not, constitute your entire spelling program. Only a portion of the words children learn during the year are learned through a routine like David's. They learn most of their reading and writing vocabulary incidentally or independently through the processes of reading and writing. You also could have routines for such activities as shared book experiences, guided reading, writing conferences, and publishing decisions. (*Specific routines related to learning phonics and spelling are explained in greater detail in Chapters 3, 4, and 5; and routines for evaluation are covered in Chapter 6.*)

Routines Allow for Intervention

As you develop structure and routines in your classroom, you will gradually shift the responsibility for some learning to your students.

For example, they should conference with each other about their reading and writing, and they should supply immediate assistance to each other when you are occupied. Also, rather than telling your students generalizations about spelling and phonics, encourage and support cooperative groups in constructing these themselves. Teaching this way frees you to move from group to group and individual to individual to provide assistance and guidance where needed. As you learn to be a kid watcher, you will be able to spend more time with the children who aren't engaged in learning or who find learning difficult, as well as those who need additional challenges. Whole language teachers soon learn to tune in to and respond to their students because they read, write, talk, and share with them. Of course, there are times when it is best for a child to have individual attention, many times when small-group work is best, and some occasions when whole-class sessions are appropriate. There are also times when inductive teaching is most effective and others when a minute or two of direct instruction is useful. As a general principle, we advise you to begin with small groups and inductive methods. As more intervention is necessary, focus in on the individual, and if an inductive approach seems less helpful for an individual, temporarily shift to more direct instruction. Whole language teachers are response teachers who acknowledge diversity and base their teaching on what their students know, not on what the teacher's handbook says. They tune in to individual needs, and they value and reward the "behavior of learning," rather than the "learned behavior."

Teachers as Learners

The whole picture of teaching and learning phonics and spelling wouldn't be complete if we didn't specifically address teachers as learners. Facilitating learners' independence and knowing how to intervene appropriately are two of the most difficult aspects of teaching, but they are essential to an effective, integrated, whole language curriculum. Therefore, move slowly into teaching in a whole language way. If the structure and routines you set up don't feel right, back up or slow down. You are probably trying to do too much too soon. You will know when it feels right. If you are unsure about your ability to be a response teacher, continue to improve your kid-watching skills, talk with colleagues, read professional materials, attend in-service workshops, and observe experienced whole language teachers. Remember, to be a whole language teacher, you must be a *learner*. Keep challenging yourself to take risks, just as you are always challenging your students to take risks.

Teaching Procedures

In the previous chapters, we said that most children will learn to read and write with no explicit instruction in phonics and spelling. Why then are we providing the following three chapters on teaching procedures? Quite simply, we believe that children need to "know what they know," have a language to talk about what they know, and be empowered to learn independently what they don't know. As a result, we feel it's important that children 1) have a language about language (metalinguistic knowledge); 2) develop strategies to learn language and learn about language while they are using language; 3) develop a have-a-go attitude; and 4) use language for communicating, learning, and living. What's more, we believe that teachers can achieve these goals during language workshops in which children learn to construct their own generalizations about language. Although young children learn and use language in all of life's situations, they may not know what they know and certainly they will not be able to express effectively and efficiently what they know about language unless someone makes the language about language explicit to them. However, through reading, writing, and responding to language, children will gain linguistic knowledge. They will also learn a language about language through activities similar to the ones described in the following three chapters.

Chapter 3

Daily Reading

As your students read authentic texts for real purposes, you will find many opportunities in which they will be able to construct their own understandings about language and how it works. It is up to you, however, to make these understandings explicit.

As you use literature and other texts, you also will be able to use many of the procedures we have included in this chapter to help your students learn graphophonic connections. The procedures employ inductive approaches that encourage risk-taking and promote discovery of language generalizations.

Sharing and Responding to Literature

During daily reading workshops, your students will be reading various texts, and the following example will show you how they can focus on reading for meaning while still learning phonics and spelling. In this illustration, second-grade teacher Helen Farthing used a shared text, *Possum Magic*, by Mem Fox (Harcourt Brace Jovanovich, 1983), a favorite piece of children's literature.

Making Connections with Literature

Because her students had enjoyed many of Mem Fox's other books, Helen was sure that this book would also be a favorite. Although many of her students were reading independently, there were still a few novice and emergent readers in the group. As a result, Helen decided that a shared book approach with the whole class would be appropriate. After introducing *Possum Magic*, Helen responded to the excited comments of the children who had already seen or heard the book, and then she quickly went on to read it with expression and enthusiasm. Although she stopped and responded to the children's comments and questions, she kept her pauses brief because she wanted to read the whole story before she actively encouraged oral responses and questions.

The students' subsequent discussion took some time because they talked about characters, their favorite parts, their own experiences with possums, and the illustrations—especially the way Julie Vivas used ghosted outlines for the invisible Hush. After several children added comments about other Mem Fox books, a few asked if they could read the book again. This time Helen invited them to read along with her. Afterwards, as the children identified the Australian animals, cities, and foods, she listed them on a piece of chart paper and hung it at eye level.

Later during reading time, Helen made copies of the book available. Two children laid down on the floor with the big book, several pairs of children read from the library's two hardback copies, and several of the small versions (published as companions to the big book) were chosen by children who tucked themselves away in

continued

Snapshot *continued*

the reading corner for some quiet reading time. Three children spontaneously gathered in the art corner after reading the book to make stick puppets, an activity they had done as a class-response activity with a previous book. One made Hush, one made Grandma Poss, and one designed a ghostly figure of Hush. Afterwards, they went off to write a script for their puppet play.

Because Helen wanted to introduce one small group to story mapping, she prepared a map of Australia, which she traced from an overhead image projected onto a large sheet of paper. Then she distributed a set of atlases and asked the children if they could find any of the places named in *Possum Magic*. Together they used this information to mark on the map the places that Grandma Poss and Hush visited in their search for the right foods.

Over the next few days, Helen captured magic moments for skill development by conducting a series of lessons using *Possum Magic*. She planned instruction in the building of word families by beginning with rhyming words from the book and 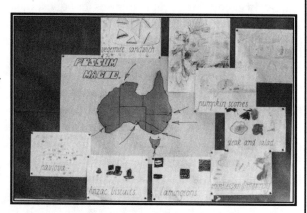 then brainstorming others. The children offered such words as *pink, shrink, think, stink, link, mink, rink, sink,* and *wink*. At one point, when Martin suggested the word *zinc*, the following exchange took place.

> **Helen:** Yes, *zinc* certainly rhymes with the words on our list. Let me write it here on the chalkboard so we can have a look. (She wrote *zink*.) Could that be right?

> **Children:** (There was general agreement that her spelling could be correct.)

continued

Snapshot *continued*

     Helen: Listen to the sound at the end of our list of words. What other letter could we use for that sound?

     Children: It could be a *c*.

     Helen: Right! We actually spell *zinc* like this. (She wrote *zinc* on the board to the right of the *-ink* word list.)

     Then Helen continued her instruction with the building of words that contained the *-ink* cluster by adding suffixes and prefixes to form words such as *stink, stinks, stinker, stinking; think, thinks, thinking,* and *unthinking.*

     Two days later, she asked a small group of children with whom she was working to find and list all words containing the /ŏ/ sound (traditionally referred to as the "short o" sound) in *Possum Magic*. They found the following words. As the children called them out, Helen wrote them on a chart.

upon	not	possums	Poss
wombats	of	squashed	from
what	on	body	stop
because*	squashed*	want*	was*
crossed*			

*__NOTE:__ The examples used here were identified by Australian children living in Melbourne. Because the classifications were made according to their dialect, some will be different for children from other English-speaking countries. You may even have dialect differences within your classroom which would result in a single word being classified differently.

continued

Snapshot *continued*

Helen and her students then classified the words above according to the spelling for the /ŏ/ sound as follows.

o	upon	not	possums
	Poss	wombats	of
	from	crossed	on
	body	stop	
a	squashed	what	was
au	because		

Helen then wrote the words on the following chart, which included words containing the /o/ sound that they had started some weeks earlier. (Similar charts can include words that have the same sound but different spellings for that sound. See pages 148-152 in the Appendix for a complete listing of the phonic elements and possible spellings.)

Helen linked these activities to *Possum Magic* because these skills, which her students needed, were more meaningful when learned in context. Although she wants the children to be hooked on books, she also wants them to have the skills they will need to become lifelong readers and writers.

/ŏ/

o	ŏ	pot
	o		a

o		a
lot dot		what
hot moth		yacht
octopus top		squashed
knot coffee		was
		ow
not October		
froth clock		
frost coffin		**ou**
nod flock		cough
upon possums		
Poss wombats		**au**
of from		
crossed on		auction
body stop		because

48

Possibilities: More Magic Moments

Since all text is language, all texts have numerous possibilities for highlighting different aspects of language. There is no need to milk a book dry of skills and bore your students in the process; it is better to use the skills possibilities available in a variety of literature and other authentic texts. However, to consider further possibilities for *Possum Magic*, we describe below alternative activities used by Marilyn Perry, another second-grade teacher. She chose different phonics and spelling patterns from *Possum Magic* because her children's needs were different.

Letter and Sound Search. One of the activities that Marilyn had her students do was to list words in *Possum Magic* that contain the letter *a*.

a	ago	ames	grandma
made	all	and	magic
kookaburra	that	was	what
adventure	because	squashed	safe
had	wombats	snakes	koala

Then she and her students categorized the list according to the letter-sound relationships.

à	(æ)	gr<u>a</u>ndma <u>a</u>nd	m<u>a</u>gic th<u>a</u>t	w<u>o</u>mbats
ä	(el)	n<u>a</u>mes sn<u>a</u>kes	m<u>a</u>de pl<u>a</u>ce	s<u>a</u>fe d<u>a</u>y
ó	(o)	w<u>a</u>s* squ<u>a</u>shed*	wh<u>a</u>t	bec<u>au</u>se*

continued

ù	(ʌ)	a*	ago*	kookaburra*
		koala*		
ar	(a:)	grandma	koala	
or	(:)	all		

*NOTE: These classifications were made by the children in Marilyn's class. Dialect differences will determine how children classify the sounds. Linguistically, the vowel sound in *a, ago, kookaburra,* and *koala* is actually the schwa sound.

As you do this activity in your classroom, keep in mind that your goal is to help your students learn about patterns of spelling. You shouldn't be overly concerned about differences in sound or correctness in the classification of the sound.

Other Skill Activities. Marilyn also decided to have her students focus on word endings, contractions, and opposites. The important point to consider when doing activities like these is that by helping your students learn about letters and the sounds they represent, they will become better spellers.

Word Endings:	squashed	looked	shouted
	remained	crossed	breathed
	appeared	waited	danced
	closed	worked	nibbled
Contractions:	couldn't	wasn't	don't
	can't	we'll	they'd
	let's		
Opposites:	visible/invisible	expected/unexpected	

Activities with Initial Letters for K–1

The previous activities are appropriate during the second half of grade 1 and higher, but there are different activities—still based on *Possum Magic*—you could use for kindergarten through the first half of grade 1.

K-1 Activities

Gayle Baker chose the following passage from *Possum Magic*.

> *Later, on a beach in Perth, they ate a piece of pavlova.*
> *Hush's legs appeared.*
> *So did her body.*
> *"You look wonderful you precious possum!" said Grandma Poss.*
>   *"Next Stop—Tasmania."*
> *And over the sea they went.*

Then she wrote the following words from that passage on a chart.

Perth
piece of pavlova
precious possum

With these words, her students then composed the following tongue twister, which they all had fun trying to say quickly.

The precious possum had a piece of pavlova in Perth.

Gayle then began the following chart of words beginning with *p*, and during the next few days she added other *p* words. She included the *p* words from the story at the beginning of the chart—even though she didn't expect these words to become sight words for her early-primary level children.

Pp		
Perth	pavlova	precious
possum	Patrick	party
puppy	Paul	pink

contiuned

Snapshot continued

Because poetry often contains alliteration, Gayle purposely selected poems that contain a high incidence of the letter *p* to read to her children, to further draw their attention to this letter. For example, after reading "Peter, Peter Pumpkin Eater" and the Southern American folk song "The Pawpaw Patch," her students added the following words to the class's chart of words starting with *p*.

Peter, Peter, Pumpkin Eater

Peter, Peter, Pumpkin eater
Had a wife and couldn't keep her.
Put her in a pumpkin shell
And there he kept her very well.

Traditional

Peter	pumpkin	pretty	pawpaw
picking	putting	pocket	patch

Eventually Gayle hung the letter chart on the wall—at the children's eye level—to encourage them to continue to add words on their own. The class made the following two charts.

Aa			Mm	
They ate Anzac biscuits in Adelaide			Mornay and Minties in Melbourne	
Anzac	ate	act	Mornay	Minties
Adelaide	Andy	acorn	Melbourne	munch
ape	add	animal	Monday	Morn

Following are some other activities that will help your students learn the letters of the alphabet and initial letter-sound correspondence. Knowing the names of the letters is necessary metalinguistic knowledge if children are going to be able to talk about their language.

The Alphabet Song and ABC Rhymes

For what seems like ages, children have learned the names of the letters by singing "The Alphabet Song," but sometimes they form misconceptions from singing the song. The most common misconception is the belief that "l-m-n-o" is all one letter. To avoid such potential problems, make a chart of the song so that your students can point to the letters as they sing. By pointing to the letters, they will learn a one-to-one correspondence with the letter names and the letters they represent. There are also numerous jump-rope rhymes and other alphabet games that your students can sing and play. One that is great fun for kids as they begin developing initial letter-sound knowledge is "B my name is Barbara; my brother's name is Bob. We build bridges and we live in Boston." This pattern continues throughout the alphabet. An added benefit is the need for your students to learn geographical place names in order to play.

First-Letter Dictionaries

You also may want to use the "The Alphabet Song" to introduce your students to first-letter dictionaries, in which they match key words from literature and their own personal experiences with each letter of the alphabet. You can help your students create their own first-letter dictionaries by using a double page for each letter. Next, print several key words or sample words associated with a picture (or pictures) on the left-hand page. Then let your students use the right-

hand page to develop their own personal entries. You also may want to have a page for each of the following consonant digraphs: *ch, ph, sh, th,* and *wh* and extra pages for special entries such as topic words, number words, and days of the week. Then, to personalize their dictionaries, they can include pictures of their families, friends, and homes.

When kindergarten children want to add words to their dictionaries, encourage them to bring their dictionaries to you (or a parent helper or cross-age tutor), opened to the correct page. Depending on their development, they can write their own words, or you can write their words for them. Whatever your students' level, encourage them to add to their dictionaries any time they come across words they want to remember from their reading. Once students have learned to use temporary spellings effectively, they'll find that their dictionaries come in handy for checking what they have written. However, as we mentioned before, it's usually best that students don't use their dictionary while they are writing, so they don't interrupt the flow of their thoughts and ideas.

Alphabet Boxes

To make alphabet boxes, which are another form of the first-letter dictionary, cut down milk cartons or any other such boxes, cover them with adhesive plastic, and label each one with a different letter of the alphabet—including both upper- and lowercase.

Then over the following weeks, choose key words from literature or from your students' writing, write the words on index cards, and place them in the appropriate boxes. For example, after your students have written a wall story together, you might choose key words from their story and place the words in the alphabet boxes. (Wall stories are composed and illustrated by students on butcher paper and then hung on the wall for a week or so. Wall stories can then be stapled into big books for later enjoyment.) You might also add key words to the boxes from any shared literature, a social studies or science unit, favorite songs and poems, or even recipes.

Later you can have your students work in pairs or in small groups to reclassify the words in the alphabet boxes—reading and using them as they sort. If you do this activity, you should always have blank boxes covered with a laminated surface available so that your students can create additional categories for sorting words.

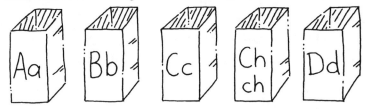

ABC Books

You can create a whole-class ABC book just by collecting words from your students' daily work-in-progress and writing them into a book of large stapled pages. Your students could then cut out or draw pictures to accompany the words. (You may want to use Graeme Base's *Animalia* [1986] as a model.) For another alternative, make a book for only one letter, such as *Our B Book*. Have the single-letter book center on a specific topic such as animals, or just fill it with *B* pictures and words your students find in magazines. Another idea is to make an ABC book on a topic your class is studying science or social studies.

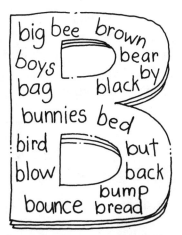

Essential Strategies at All Levels

Many whole language teachers consider the following strategies to be essential for focusing on graphophonic connections. Cloze procedures, for example, help children use semantics and syntax to develop their use of graphophonic cues. Teachers use word sorts to help children classify words from the text they have already read and responded to in some way. Both of these strategies help children form important generalizations about language that they will be able to apply to future reading and writing.

Cloze

Teachers who want their students to develop graphophonic knowledge often use cloze procedures to focus on certain letters, letter clusters, and/or letter patterns. Usually, they cover certain letters with a mask or delete the letters from the text. Then, to create meaning, their students read the text and predict the missing letters.

> **Example:** Paul brought his pet _og to school.
> It was _agging its tai_ and bark_ _ _ .

You also can use stick-on notes to cover letters or groups of letters in a big book or on a chart. In the following example, children must draw on their knowledge of consonants in initial and final positions and the *-ing* ending. You can use the same technique to highlight different inflectional endings or common letter clusters.

Paul br_ _ _ _t his pet dog to scho_ _. It was wagging its t_ _l and b_ _king	Paul brought his pet d_ _ to school. It was wag_ _ _ _ its _ _ _ _ and _ _ _ _ _ _ _.
Using beginning and ending cues	**Using semantic and syntactic cues**

You can use the cloze procedure with poetry. For example, try using stick-on notes or a sliding mask to cover the endings of words that are highly predictable from their context. A benefit of this procedure is that you can tailor it to your students' needs and developmental levels because you can make activities easier or more difficult, depending on which letter clusters you choose to omit or mask.

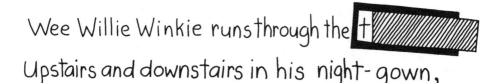

Wee Willie Winkie runs through the t[   ]

Upstairs and downstairs in his night-gown,

Word Sorts

Word sorts involve grouping words into categories to help children form generalizations about graphophonic, syntactic, or semantic features. To begin, have your students write words they already know on small cards, or let them copy words from their alphabet boxes or first-letter dictionaries. Then have them sort the words according to their initial letters. (Pocket charts often make sorting easier for young children.) Once your students have mastered initial letters, you can show them alternative ways to sort by defining various criteria for sorting. For example, after several readings of Mary Austin's poem "Grizzly Bear" (in Powell & Butler, 1989a), you might write the following words on cards.

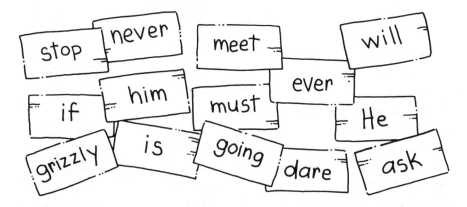

After you place the words on a table next to a pocket chart, ask your students to sort the words into long-vowel words and short-vowel words.

Short Vowels			Long Vowels	
If	ever	grizzly	meet	He
must	stop	is	going	dare
will	ask	him		
never				

57

Then as your students gain confidence, encourage them to develop their own criteria for sorting. For example, they could decide to sort the words above by looking for those that contain the letter *m*, by finding the short *i* sound, or by identifying words that have one or two syllables. For those who need an even bigger challenge, suggest sorting by more than one criterion.

Cluster Analysis

Research shows that effective readers look at clusters or chunks of information—especially beginning and ending clusters—when reading unfamiliar words (Goswami & Bryant, 1990). These clusters consist of letter combinations that make certain sounds in certain words. Pulvertaft (1978, p. 38) describes cluster analysis and emphasizes that during the procedure, it's important for children to remember that the same letter combinations do not always represent the same sounds. However, understanding the beginning and ending clusters, combined with predictions based on meaning and syntax, readers are able

to decode words they have not seen in print before. This process also helps them build relationships for remembering spelling patterns.

Brief sessions of cluster analysis can be beneficial to many of your students. In fact, cluster analysis may help all of them become aware of a new way of thinking about words and may give them a way to tackle unfamiliar words. They won't all need your help to use this knowledge in a practical way because many will be able to develop their own strategies for using their knowledge. Nevertheless, once you observe how your students are operating as readers and writers, you

58

should determine which ones would benefit from cluster analysis sessions. As always, keep the sessions brief.

Classroom Snapshot

Cluster Analysis

A spontaneous example of cluster analysis occurred in Helen's second-grade classroom because her students took a keen interest in her aquarium. Trent, who spent considerable time watching the fish and talking about them, often wished that he had some pet fish. As a result, he collected information about aquarium fish and wrote a report that he shared with the class. (He also wrote a letter to his parents, asking them if he could have an aquarium for his birthday.) The class was quite interested in Trent's report, and afterwards several other children decided that they were also going to ask their parents for an aquarium. Helen used this interest to select key words from Trent's report containing the -*ish* cluster because she knew that the sample words should always come from some work-in-progress so that they can be related back to the text.

Cluster: -*ish*

Sample word: *fish*

Helen: This word is *fish*. In the word *fish*, which letter stands for the /f/ sound? Which letters stand for the /ish/ sound? In the word *fish*, what sound does the letter *f* stand for? What sound do the letters *i-s-h* stand for?

Note: This procedure is repeated for two or three /ish/ words.

Cluster analysis can also help some children make connections. For example, if they know the words *truck* and *face*, they may be in a much better position to get the word *trace*. You can turn this activity into a game by encouraging your students to make new words from the beginnings and endings of other words. (You should, however, use this procedure with caution as it may be more confusing to some children than helpful.)

A Routine for Essential Strategies

Mary McDonald (1992) built several of the above strategies into a routine that she calls "Rhyme Reading." Her routine is most useful for children up to fourth grade, but it is especially useful for many kinds of special readers: for nonconfident readers; readers who have failed to build up a basic sight vocabulary; students from non-English-speaking backgrounds; and readers who overemphasize one reading strategy at the expense of others.

If you want to use this routine, you can begin by making three large copies of a well-known rhyme. Put one copy aside for group use, cut up the second copy into sentence strips, and cut up the third copy into words. You may want to begin by teaching the rhyme orally with such techniques as clapping or other body actions that emphasize the rhyme and rhythm.

When you introduce the rhyme on the first chart, run your finger under the words as you read them so that directional conventions and aural-visual matching occur. Then have different children read the rhyme, or you can help group members take different parts or read alternate lines. Afterwards, have your students sequence the sentence strips made from the second copy.

At the beginning of a second session, enjoy the rhyme together by chanting, clapping, stamping, or choral reading it. Then reread the rhyme and focus on matching spoken words with printed words. You can accomplish this by playing a game in which you nominate a word, and then your students clap every time you read that word. Follow this activity by covering some of the words on the chart and then having your students supply the missing words as they read the rhyme.

During a third session, you might choose words that have common letters or letter clusters for cluster analysis. Then your students should use the word cards made from the third copy to build the rhyme. You also could have them write an innovation on the text or sort the words of the rhyme according to letters or letter clusters. Later you could use this same rhyme for identifying rhyming words and using them to build word families and for letter searches and sound searches.

As each rhyme is introduced, an individual copy is pasted into each child's Rhyme Book. Once a set of well-known rhymes is collected, it becomes a favorite to take home and read to others. The children can also have fun mixing up parts of the rhymes for their friends to sort.

Becoming Word Watchers

In order for children to tune in to the meaning and spelling of new words, they need to develop a genuine interest in words. Rather than having students look up words in the dictionary before every story they read, you could use some or all of the following activities—sometimes in conjunction with reading and sometimes during a content area study—to create an interest in and better understanding of words.

Chants and Rhymes

If you have ever listened to children on a playground, you have heard them chanting and making up rhymes of their own. They tease each other in chants, chant as they jump rope, and babble to themselves in chants and rhymes. Many of these word plays have been handed down for many years, but others are original. A good idea is to write down any chants or rhymes you hear your students saying, or actually have them dictate them to you. You also could explore Sonja Dunn's two books of chants and rhymes for ones you think your students would like (*Butterscotch Dreams*, 1987 and *Crackers and Crumbs*, 1990). You can use these chants and rhymes for studying spelling patterns.

Tongue Twisters and Alliterations

A favorite way of ours to get children to tune in to initial sounds is through tongue twisters and alliterations. After reading "Peter Piper picked a peck of pickled peppers," for example, few children will have any difficulty recognizing the initial sound of *p*.

I Spy

A popular game that children can play on their own or in the classroom is "I Spy." To begin, one child should say, "I spy with my little eye something beginning with *d.*" (This child could also have used medial sounds or ending sounds.) Then the other children should take turns guessing what it is. After someone gives a wrong guess, the first child should respond by saying, "Yes, that begins with *d,* but the thing I see is on the wall" (or another such clue). The first person must continue to supply clues until the word is guessed correctly.

Sound Charts

Poetry is an excellent source of words for word studies. If your students seem to be confused by the multiple spelling patterns for the /k/ sound, for example, you may find that using the nursery rhyme "Hickory Dickory Dock" would be helpful if they can locate all of the words in the poem that contain the /k/ sound. Once they have found all of the words, they should then categorize them according to their spelling pattern.

> **Hickory dickory dock**
> **The mouse ran up the clock**
> **The clock struck one**
> **The mouse ran down**
> **Hickory dickory dock**

As you read more poetry and other forms of literature, your students should locate other /k/ words and categorize them by their spelling patterns. (A complete list of phonic elements and sample sound charts are included on pages 148-152 in the Appendix) Soon you should see that your students are being motivated to locate words for less common spelling patterns such as *qu, cc,* and *ch.* Also, after considerable practice with sound charts, your students should begin to categorize words and make generalizations on their own.

Homophone Pairs

Homophones—words that sound the same but have different meanings and spellings—are examples of words that are not learned solely with graphophonic strategies, but also with visual and meaning strategies. After your students have read a text, refer them back into it to find homophone pairs. (The various pairs should be listed on a class chart.) Once the chart has built up over time, write the individual words on cards, which your students can use to play a matching game by shuffling and dealing the cards. Each student, in turn, should take a card from the player on his or her right. Eventually, when a child has a matching pair, he should put it down on the table. The first one with no cards is the winner. This game will help your students focus on different spelling patterns for the same sound.

Homophones		
sum/some	new/knew	hear/here
sea/see	flew/flue	to/too/two
there/their/they're	by/buy/bye	wait/weight

Silent Letter Search

Ask your students to search quickly through various reading materials and their own writing for words that contain silent letters. After everyone has contributed to the list and it is long enough, have your students group the words according to spelling patterns such as the following:

knee	write	comb	sign	gnaw
know	wrong	lamb	design	gnu
knit	wring	bomb	benign	gnome
knife	wrinkle	limb	resign	

Once you have compiled your list of words into word families, you will be able to help your students not only understand why some of these letters are silent but also why they are there in the first place. For example, in the word family *sign/signal/signature*, the *g* is pronounced in the latter two derivations. (Studying the etymology of words can be interesting and can shed light on unusual spelling patterns.) When you help your students to make these kinds of links, you are helping them to remember the spellings of these words. At the same time, you will be showing them that spelling is not a hit-or-miss proposition—rather, there are often reasons for the unexpected spellings of certain words.

Roots of Language

Although the English language is made up of many words with Latin and Greek roots, many others have been borrowed from other languages—such as German, French, Indian, Scandinavian, and Chinese. Your students will be able to increase their knowledge of words and better understand the spelling patterns if they learn more about the derivation of words. Looking at groups of words that belong together in meaning not only helps young spellers develop their morphemic knowledge, but it also helps them to understand why certain words are spelled the way they are. For example, a study of the following group of words should help children understand that the letter *c* is part of the root and represents the /s/ sound in *medicine* and *medicinal* because the *c* is followed by an *i*.

*medic*ine   *medic*al   *medic*o
*medic*inal   *medic*ation

The common root in each word helps the reader to tie these words together in meaning. Since English spelling reflects meaning as well as sound, such an activity can help children read these words more easily. Other Latin and Greek roots and their derivatives can be used on charts to help your students learn the common relationships in both meaning and spelling. However, you should point out that some roots have variations in their spelling.

Ped			
*ped*estrian	*pod*iatrist	*ped*dle	*pod*iatry
*ped*igree	*pod*ium	*ped*al	*ped*icure

English Word	Derived From	Related Words
manipulate	Latin *manus* = hand	manual, manicure, manufacture, maneuver
explain	Latin *explanare* = to make smooth	explainable explanation, explanatory
kumquat	Chinese *kam* = gold + *quat* = orange	

Portmanteau Words

Sometimes closely related words are combined to form one word. For example, *br*eakfast + *lunch* = brunch. Following are more examples of these words, which are called *portmanteau words*.

Portmanteau Word	Base Words
smog	smog + fog
motel	motor + hotel
telecast	television + broadcast

A study of portmanteau words can help your students see how new words are created by combining parts of existing words and how known spelling patterns can be combined. Once they are familiar with portmanteau words, encourage students to create some of their own.

Word Webs

Words with related meanings often have similar spelling patterns. By graphically making the connections among words from the same root, you can make some important spelling connections.

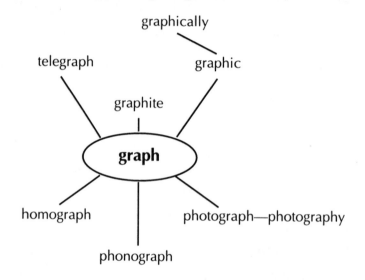

Keeping Reading Activities in Perspective

After you become comfortable drawing attention to graphophonic and spelling patterns in the context of literature and other authentic texts, you will make up your own teaching activities to accommodate the needs of your children and your school curriculum. As we have said before, take the lead from the children, keep the activities brief, keep them in context as much as possible, and ask yourself why it is important for your students to learn this skill. You should always see the direct link to reading and writing or the skill probably isn't worth learning.

Chapter 4

DAILY WRITING

> hildren would never need to learn to spell if they were never going to write. When teachers put meaning first and help young writers communicate what they want to say, spelling becomes a consequence of learning to write.

When children are doing the suggested activities in this chapter, it's likely that much of the time they won't even recognize that they're doing spelling. Yet students are putting spelling patterns into their linguistic storehouses. Since spelling in your whole language classroom won't always stand out as a separate activity, you may need to tell parents and administrators, as well as the children, when you are drawing attention to spelling. Likewise, you will need to carefully document children's growth and development in spelling because students, their parents, and administrators can easily miss it. Chapter 6 will help you to systematically document your students' progress.

Spelling While Writing Authentic Texts

A good writing program focuses first and foremost on helping children to become confident and competent writers—with all of the skills and abilities that this requires. One of the skills necessary for your students to achieve this goal, of course, is the ability to spell the words they want to use when communicating through writing. Another important skill is having the strategies that allow them to continue to draft even when they are unsure of various spellings.

When children are writing their first drafts, the generation of their ideas and the flow of their words are most important. Therefore, you should encourage them to record their ideas on paper regardless of their ability to attend to the "surface features" of written language, such as spelling, handwriting, and punctuation. However, it is through this very process of writing that they will become aware of the need to attend to these surface features, and it is always much easier to assist in the learning process when the learners themselves see the need for what they are learning.

Using Students' Texts as Models

Using examples of your students' own written texts for demonstrations of revision and proofreading skills can be an extremely helpful teaching tool because young writers get valuable suggestions and ideas from their peers that they can then use to improve their own writing. What's more, as your students are helping each other, you will be able to make optimal use of your time for teaching and giving special assistance to those who need one-on-one instruction. To use children's texts as models, of course, requires that you create a positive and cooperative learning atmosphere in your classroom. The writers in your classroom will need to know that any public exhibition of their work is only for productive purposes and that you will be using their work to help both the writer and the audience improve their writing. When these conditions are fulfilled, the use of material written by members of your classroom writing community for demonstration purposes will be most successful.

Modeling Your Own Writing

You may choose to write something on the chalkboard or on an overhead transparency to model important aspects of the writing process for the class. However, you don't want them to see only the first drafts. You want them to see your revisions in progress, as well. Rather than contriving a piece of writing just for modeling writing strategies and behaviors, think about all of the writing you do in a week, such as the following:

- **recount** of what happened during a school or classroom event
- **memo** to another teacher
- **note** to a friend
- **letter** to parents or friends
- **report** about something your students are studying in another subject area
- **story** (narrative) based on a personal experience
- **recipe** for a favorite dish
- **poem** about something familiar
- **outline** of what you want your students to do during the afternoon

Because many of the decisions that writers make as they write are silent thought processes, you should think aloud as you write for the class. This way, students will be able to listen in on the inner workings of a writer's mind. As they listen, they will hear such things as how you compose, what revision techniques you use, and how you make decisions about spelling and other conventions. Eventually they will learn that you, too, occasionally come across words you can't spell. Modeled writing is also an extremely useful tool for explaining and teaching writing skills and strategies, for demonstrating writing behaviors, and for revealing different attitudes toward writing, including excitement, satisfaction, and even occasional frustration. While there will be some discussion of the writing process during

69

your actual composing, it's the debriefing afterwards that usually will help your students identify and talk more about elements of the writing process and, meanwhile, learn the language about language. This language will then empower them not only to be able to write but also to be able to talk about their writing.

Using Innovations on Text

You can use familiar text, such as a well-loved nursery rhyme or poem, to provide a structure for your students' own shared writing, and the same text can also serve as a blueprint for their later independent writing. When your students participate in these shared experiences, they will learn structures for their own writing, such as rhyming patterns, double adjectives, refrains, and cause-and-effect relationships. And when children are working out rhyming words and attending to syllabication, they will also be attending to spelling patterns and graphophonic connections. To start with, if students don't always make rhymes or replace syllables in the original exactly, don't worry. They are still learning important lessons about writing. Innovations can also be done as a group activity to help children focus on particular words, and they can assist ESL children and others who are not yet comfortable with writing to take small, initial risks with their writing. Because they know what a poem says, for instance, they are tuning in to spelling patterns and the way words look as they copy the poem. They also can personalize the text by including their own words, which are added, of course, in their own spelling.

CLASSROOM
Snapshot

Innovations on Text

Jean Rachubinski, a first-grade teacher, had her students read a favoritewell-known poem, "A Thousand Hairy Savages" by Spike Milligan (from *Silly Verse for Kids*, Dobson Books Limited, 1963).

continued

Snapshot *continued*

After reading it once, she omitted key words such as hairy and savages by covering them with stick-on notes, as in oral cloze, and by replacing the words with a line.

A thousand _____ _____

The children then reread the poem, clapping the syllables they heard in the poem. Afterwards, they brainstormed other words that could replace the missing words, but that would still have the same number of syllables.

A thous-and ___-__ ___-__-___

Sit-ting down to lunch
Gob-ble gob-ble glup glup
Munch munch munch.

Following are the results that Jean got when she asked her students to think of possible words that could fit the pattern, the rhyme, and the meaning.

Innovation:

A thousand chubby teacher friends
Sitting down to lunch
Gobble gobble glup glup
Munch munch munch.

Other innovations may keep the pattern, but change the content:

A thousand little grubby kids
Playing somewhat rough
Running round the race track
Puff, puff, puff.

Writing Journals and Response Logs

Journals are not diaries or workbooks. Rather, they are a chance to engage in writing that experiments with form, style, and voice

(Fulwiler, 1987). Journal entries, which should be dated, are valuable because the more your students write from the heart, the more they will be able to connect to their audiences (and audiences make spelling important). Although journals can have many formats, the three most common types are: *responsive logs* (used to respond to a book or an experience); *learning logs* (usually used in a content study); and *dialogue journals* (used like either of the above). Dialogue journals, in which both you and a student comment upon each other's entries, push children the most to be spelling conscious.

CLASSROOM Snapshot

Grade 5 Writing Journal

André Sampson is a Grade 5 student at Ringwood Heights School in Melbourne, Australia. With a group of Grade 5 and 6 children, he read poems, novels and picture-story books that were linked by their attention to the effects of war on people's lives. They were considering the concept of "personal journeys." The literature was chosen to highlight individual acts of humanity and extreme courage shown by people in difficult and life-threatening circumstances, despite man's inhumanity to man and the horror and stupidity of war.

Extracts from André Sampson's journal include:

18 Oct. The introduction of *The Silver Sword* captures my attention greatly. It also sets enthusiasm in the reader's mind....Zakyna must have been terrifying for Joseph and anybody else. If I was there for that long with that treatment, I would have gone crazy....

19 Oct. ...It must have beeen terrible news for the father to hear from Mrs. Krause that his wife had been taken away and that his children were dead. I feel terribly sorry for him. But I think determination to find his wife and his supposedly dead children will bring him back to happiness....

continued

24 Oct. ...Terror must have overwhelmed Edek on his cold and dangerous escape under the train. I wonder what Jan feels like now?....

27 Oct. My eyes are stuck on the book! How are they going to survive the rapids?

Journals help students like André engage in authentic literacy events. For example, journals can provide avenues for such meaningful expressions as personal responses, questioning, thinking aloud on paper, reflections, diagrams and drawings, personal anecdotes, and even sudden insights. "When people write about new information and ideas—in addition to reading, talking, and listening— they learn and understand them better" (Britton, 1975).

Grade 1-2
Writing Journal

In Nadine Watson's first/second-grade class, children's journals take on the different formats that she had modeled over time. Whether the format is a letter to the teacher, a double-entry log, a diary format, or any one of many different formats, the reflective nature of writing about what has been read has a power to it that is illustrated in the following journal entries by two of her students, Kyla and Bonnie.

Dear Ms. Watson.
 I raed Nana Upstairs and Nana Downstairs. This book is ret'n and Illustratred by Tomie de Paola. I selected this book becuas you raed it to us, and I thought it was wondrful. The story is about a little boy named Tommy and his grandmother and grat-grandmother. Becuas I liked the pichers and texst. The story reminded me of my grandmother that uste to give us candy chanes and lots of cndys. She dided of lung cnser. Yes, I, would recommend this book to Kyra. Yes, ther are Tommy Nana Upstairs and Nana Downstairs. Becuas it talks about love, and famly.

 Love,
 Bonnie

continued

Snapshot *continued*

After Kyla took Bonnie's recommendation and read *Nana Upstairs, Nana Downstairs*, she responded with the following journal entry.

The spelling in these two journal entries is fairly conventional because when children are invested in their message, they are more likely to attend to spelling. Your written comments in students' journals also provide multiple demonstrations of language in use. For example, your students usually have many opportunities to compare their attempts to spell a word (temporary spellings) with the conventionally correct form that appears in your entries. Although this main purpose of journal writing should never be for the teaching of spelling, these are, nevertheless, valuable fringe benefits.

Kyra
One morning when Tommy woke up at his own house, his mother came in to talk to him. "Nana Upstairs died last night," she said.

Nana Upstairs and Nana Downstairs by Tomie de Paola. The sentince reminds me of when my mom came into my room and said your dad died last night My dad died of secyers he was driveing along the road and sodenly he had a secrer, and he hit his head on the stering wheel and it noct him out The next day he was found dead he did not have any blod presier, that night I cried and cried and cried.

Written Conversations

Written conversations are simply conversations on paper between two writers: teacher and child, child and child, child and cross-age tutor, or even child and parent. Written conversations are usually nonthreatening because they focus on what two people want to say, rather than on the surface features of the written language. As a result, they are particularly useful with reluctant writers and those students who lack confidence as writers because they force these students to take risks with spelling by using whatever strategies they know. Because this process is much like an oral conversation, there isn't time for proofreading or asking questions about spelling. As a result, each participant reads what the other has written and learns from that. If you are one of the participants, then these reluctant writers and/or poor spellers will be able to make some comparisons between their spelling and yours without being told theirs is incorrect. Written conversations can also be useful for children who are lackadaisical about spelling and are rarely concerned about making their spelling approximations as close as possible to the conventional forms. The impact for them comes with the immediate feedback they get from their partners.

Using Have-a-Go Strategies

While drafting a piece of writing, many young writers lack the strategies needed for attempting temporary spellings of words they want to use. As a result, they can become stuck on one word, thereby disrupting their flow of ideas. That's why it's important that you share with your students various strategies, like the following, that they can use to have a go. Of course, such strategies will make more sense to your students if you can provide them with examples from their own writing. It's important that you are explicit about the skills and strategies you are modeling.

- **Write the first letter or first-letter cluster and then follow it with a dash.**

At the zoo, I saw the lins. It was danj— when the man wet in to feed thm. He was brav.

- **Leave out any letters in question and replace them with a dash.**

On Sat-day I went to the baseball game.

- **Underline or circle any word or part of a word that needs to be checked later.**

Dear Mrs. Hornsby
I'm going to my Nans nekst week. She has lots of rosalers at her farm.
        from Felicity

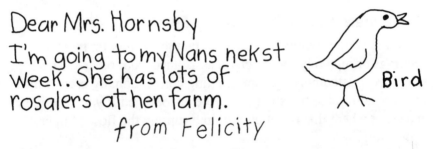

Bird

   Felicity chose to label her drawing "Bird" since she was unsure of the spelling of "rosella"!

- **Recall what a word looks like and then use what you know about sounds and letters.**

I like my dog. He is an alsashun.

- **Draw a picture of any word in question.**

Wuns there was a little old w

If your students use these strategies as they are drafting, their thoughts and ideas will not get bogged down by having to stop and check the spelling of various words. These strategies can also offer you insights into the spelling and graphophonic knowledge your students have when you study patterns of their usage over time. Another way to develop confident spellers and model the risk-taking necessary for creative writers is to invite your students to have a go with you. In other words, when you are about to write a word that you don't think your students can spell, ask them to offer suggestions while you write them on the chalkboard or on a chart. Then take one of their suggestions and underline it so you can go back to it and check it during the following editing. This kind of positive modeling will show your students that it's okay to take some risks when drafting a piece of writing.

Willingness to Use Temporary Spellings

Some young writers may be reluctant to attempt temporary spellings or may rely too much on assistance from others or from references. Attempts to get the spelling conventionally correct the first time are admirable but should only be encouraged if young writers are at a stage where this is not unduly interrupting the flow of their composing.

If children cannot produce an appropriate letter, encourage them to check with others or to check available references (class word lists, class charts, alphabet, and so on). If assistance is not available immediately, teach children to leave a space, draw a line, or give an "educated guess" so that they can proceed with what they want to write. The more young children learn about sound-symbol relationships in their *reading* program, the more they will be able to use that knowledge when attempting to spell the words they want to use. We don't recommend the use of have-a-go cards, dictionaries, or word banks at this time because writing (composing) is more important at this stage; you don't want the flow of writing to be interrupted.

For some children, an overconcern about spelling is not caused by any spelling problem they may have; rather, it is the result of a misguided attitude towards learning or a misunderstanding of the nature of efficient learning. Encourage these perfectionists (or prod them) to take risks. Temporary spelling serves several purposes. Firstly, children learn to write whatever they are thinking rather than only words they can spell, thus enhancing their ability to communicate meaning. Secondly, children's attempts to spell help you and the student to know how much the child knows about spelling. Thirdly, older and more experienced writers (including adults) also use temporary spellings. They may write just the first letter or two and then add a dash. These are efficient strategies for all writers. Adults certainly don't bother to get up and find a dictionary when they are drafting: that can be done later. If adults allow themselves these privileges—if professional writers write this way—then teachers must also allow children to do the same.

For students who won't take risks, we recommend that you don't usually spell words for them. Insist that they spell words the way they sound or look, but also assure them that you will help them with those words when they have finished their piece. If they are older writers, help them to understand the idea of *first draft*. Model for these children your own atttempts at temporary spelling while you write a first draft. Respond to their attempts at spelling in the following ways.

- "I love that word; it tells me just how you felt."
- "Imagine getting that word right. How did you do that?"
- "All the letters you've written are exactly right. You've left one letter out; do you know where that would go? Do you know what letter would go there?"
- "It was smart to use *ee* in that word. Have a look at this chart and see if you can remember which other letters we use for that sound."

Whole language teachers are response teachers, and occasionally there may be individual students who will resist writing unless they know how to spell the words they want to use. While the above strategies generally work, it may also be necessary to negotiate further assistance for these rare children. For example, you, a parent helper, or a cross-age tutor may write a negotiated amount of the text (for example, every second sentence). You may agree to act as scribe after the children have written a paragraph or so by themselves. It may be as simple as having a more confident speller friend or writing partner sitting close by so that assistance is always at hand. But these responses should be viewed as short-term responses; the aim is to have children develop enough confidence so that they are prepared to use temporary spellings and write independently.

Introducing Have-a-Go Cards

Have-a-go cards provide a chance for your students to try alternative spellings, but the cards are also central to their proofreading and personalized spelling instruction. In Chapter 2, we explained how have-a-go cards can be used during editing to encourage children to take risks with their spelling and to try out possible spelling patterns based on phonic connections, visual memory, and morphemic units. We have also found it best to introduce have-a-go cards when children are displaying clusters of writing behaviors and strategies that are typical in the novice stage of development. (*See pages 23-27 and 101-103 for more information about the various stages of writing development.*)

Making Have-a-Go Cards

When preparing have-a-go cards, include at least three columns. In the first column, students should transcribe temporary spellings from the work-in-progress. This column can serve as a record for comparison later on. The second column is for your students' additional attempts at spelling the words correctly, and you or a helper should use the third column for transcribing the conventional spelling of the words in question. At some point, you may even want to add a fourth column, in which your students will copy the correct spellings. (*For a sample have-a-go card, see page 38 in Chapter 2.*) Because there are many other ways to prepare have-a-go cards, you'll have the flexibility to come up with a format that best meets your students' spelling needs. You may even want to encourage your students to make suggestions for different formats and then to discuss the benefits of each.

Helping Children Have a Go

As a general rule, you or a helper should provide as much assistance as possible to help your spellers have another go on their cards, but generally, you shouldn't provide the correct spelling until it's clear that they won't arrive at it by themselves. Following are some of the different ways, that you can encourage your young spellers as they have a go.

1. Check off the letters in the word that are correct:

b l o o   (blue)

2. Tell your student that a letter is (or some letters are) missing. Then ask her to tell you where the missing letter might go and what it might be:

w e t   (went)

3. Refer the student to a similar word that he already knows how to spell. For instance, if he writes *bote* for the word *boat*, you might suggest that he think of the word *goat*.

4. Help your students use visual memory to arrive at a spelling pattern that looks right. For example, if a student is trying to spell *hum*, suggest the words *come, plum,* and *numb*. Then ask, "Which spelling pattern would most likely look right: *home, hum,* or *humb?*"

5. Refer the student to a chart, wall story, or display that contains the word she is trying to spell.

6. Refer the student to a recently read book that contains the word by saying, "We had that word in our story yesterday. Go and see if you can find it."

7. Refer the student to other possible resources, such as an atlas, map, or street directory for place names; newspapers, magazines, or encyclopedias for spellings of famous people's names; or newspapers or the *TV Guide* for the names of television shows.

8. If the student seems ready, refer her to a dictionary, but first try the strategies above.

Proofreading for Spelling

Once writers are happy with the meaning of what they've written, it's time for them to think about publishing their work. But first they must proofread their work for surface features, particularly spelling, grammar, and punctuation. If you model how to edit, or proofread, it will be easier for your students to understand and follow the process with their own writing. However, unless children are really engaged in the piece they are writing and have invested considerable time in the actual writing and revision of the piece, they are not likely to put forth the effort necessary for careful proofreading. Proofreading, of course, is never as easy as some students think it is. In fact, competent readers who sample the text and predict using minimal cues actually use strategies that detract from efficient proofreading. For example, effective proofreading strategies require the proofreader to check spelling by examining individual letters, and this process naturally slows reading down. Proofreading also requires the writer to check grammar and punctuation, which makes automatic behaviors conscious and more considered.

Proofreading should begin as soon as children start writing for audiences other than themselves. By third grade, for example, children should develop general proofreading strategies that will eventually become a regular part of their writing process. Although there is no one strategy for proofreading, a few children may need you to model some very explicit steps. The following example shows one general strategy for proofreading spelling. Notice that this method actually encompasses a series of individual strategies.

Proofreading for Spelling

1. Look at each word carefully and ask, "Does it look right?" Some writers begin at the end of their piece and work backwards, checking each word so that they don't skip words by mistake as they read. Other writers use a ruler to check one line at a time as they read each word carefully.

2. Circle the words that you need to check.

3. Ask yourself, "How else could the word be spelled?" Try one or two other ways to write the word; then check it using any of the following:

    • class word charts,

    • a friend,

    • a computer spell checker,

    • a dictionary, or

    • an adult.

4. Compare any differences and note the part(s) you misspelled.

5. Ask your teacher or another adult to make sure that you've circled all of the misspelled words. If an adult isn't available, have a friend give your writing a quick check to find any other misspellings.

You should work closely with any students who consistently include numerous misspellings in their writing. For instance, you could ask them to correct only a certain number of words, say five to ten. Then gradually increase the number. Also keep in mind that proofreading is usually more effective if you allow some time to pass in between your students' writing and their proofreading. Another way to keep children interested in proofreading is to vary the proofreading task; for example, ask your students to proofread one anothers' work. Following are some other variations of proofreading that you might want to try.

Proofreading for Younger Children

At kindergarten and early first grade, children often "publish" simply by holding up their piece and reading it aloud to others. Because their peers don't actually read the text themselves, it is not necessary for them to have correct spellings. However, after young children have progressed in their spelling development, you (or other proficient spellers such as parent volunteers, aides, or cross-age tutors) may want to work individually with your students to proofread their writing with them and then transcribe the child's writing into "grown-up" spelling. If you follow this suggestion, you will quickly recognize which of your students have the skills to proofread their own work and which will need further assistance.

Noting Progress

Children should learn to check their own spelling progress every three months or so. They will, of course, need some direction from you. For example, after proofreading a particular piece of writing, a student could compare that piece with another piece he had previously proofread, looking for any progress in spelling. He might ask the following questions: How many words were misspelled in each piece? How many misspelled words did I find? How many misspellings were corrected on my first try? What changes can I see in my spelling?

It is more important for a student to try to assess *why* some pieces had more misspellings than others. Possibly the content was more difficult, or perhaps he was more tuned in to developing the structure and less focused on spelling.

Establishing Word Banks

Once your students have chosen five or so words that they'd like to learn to spell, they should enter them into personalized word banks for later practice. Students can make simple word banks by stapling a sheet of paper inside their writing or spelling notebooks and listing the words there. Later, these word banks can be added to spelling checks along with the words from their have-a-go cards.

Creating Memory Joggers

Children should keep track of frequently used words that they misspell. Then, like most adults, they can learn little tricks to help them spell these words correctly. For example, many people are able to remember the correct spelling of the word *together* by breaking it into smaller words: *to/get/her.* The clever ways of remembering how to spell a word are called mnemonics, or memory joggers. For example, to remember *principal*, you can think, "The princi*pal* is your *pal*." After a few examples, some children can come up with their own mnemonics.

Write the word you circled.	Have a go at the word.	The correct spelling of the word.	Mnemonic or Memory Jogger
heare	here	hear	I *hear* with my ear
labbratory	labratory	laboratory	Pronounce: la-bor'-a-tory

85

Keeping Writing Activities in Perspective

Spelling can be learned in the context of children's writing as well as their reading. We believe that you begin with children's temporary spelling and then negotiate how much children will learn and how they will learn best. Although spelling is learned throughout the curriculum, writing is one of the most obvious ways to observe children's graphophonic understandings and for children to have a need to spell. Activities such as those discussed in this chapter can help you to make spelling and phonics more explicit. Just as we believe that it is impossible to separate phonics from spelling and reading from writing, we believe that it is difficult to separate teaching strategies from evaluation strategies and, therefore, refer you to Chapter 6 for more information.

Chapter 5

Writing/Reading from Shared Experiences

> **T**hrough experience and through language we learn.
> Experience needs language to give it form. Language needs experience to give it content... (Hall, 1976, p. 1)

A *shared experience* occurs anytime children participate together in an event, project, field trip, discussion, demonstration, book, or any other type of experience (Ashton-Warner, 1963; Holdaway, 1979; Van Allen, 1976). From such shared experiences, children discuss, research, read, dramatize, draw, write, create, and reflect, and all shared experiences offer authentic contexts for learning phonics and spelling. As a whole language teacher, you should try to use every learning experience as a way for your students not only to develop their language but also to learn about their language. For example, as you teach science, health, and social studies with a hands-on inquiry approach, some of the richest opportunities for your students to learn language and to learn about language will occur because they will be engaged in such meaningful tasks as reading to research, writing to learn, reading nonfiction for gaining overall knowledge of a topic, and writing to publish the information they have learned. Although the learning of phonics and spelling can be somewhat subtle in such situations, we hope to show you how you can pull the language generated during such experiences into your reading-writing workshops and apply many of the teaching strategies already suggested in the first two chapters of this section to help your students learn and reinforce graphophonic connections.

In this chapter you will read about two teachers who used a trip to the zoo to create many meaningful learning experiences. (Though many of these experiences were carefully planned, spontaneous experiences also provided opportunities for language development.) By the end of the chapter, we hope that you will be convinced that natural learning cycles—both planned and spontaneous—can and should drive your curriculum.

A Trip to the Zoo

Cheryl Grambau and Zena Goodman planned a trip to the zoo with their grade 1-2 classes as an early experience in an integrated unit on animals. Before the trip, the two determined their students' understandings about the zoo by asking questions such as, "What animals will we see at the zoo?" "Who works at the zoo?" and "What do the animals eat?" Then the students made clay figures of some of the animals they predicted they'd see and classified toy animals according to those they might have as pets, those they might see only at the zoo, and those that live mainly on farms.

Expressing Understandings

After their trip, the children actively shared their experiences through a variety of artistic means, such as miming animal actions for classmates to guess, drawing pictures and making collages of what they'd seen, using instruments to make animal sounds, and making 3-

D models of the zoo and of various animals. As both teachers encouraged their students to express themselves orally during the various activities, they took advantage of every opportunity to extend

their students' vocabularies. Then through drama, art, music, and oral expression, the children expressed their understandings of the experiences they had shared, and as a result, they were able to develop the precursors to writing.

Reading and Discussing

In order to extend their students' understanding and involvement in the zoo study, Zena and Cheryl read aloud the best literature available, including nonfiction and reference books, about the zoo and zoo animals. Again, as the children listened to and discussed these books, there were not only many opportunities to develop the content but also to develop the students' vocabulary and their experiences with various uses and styles of language. Next, the children were involved in small-group discussion. As they talked about their trip to the zoo and the books that they had been reading, their teachers closely monitored their oral language and helped establish and refine their listening skills, such as waiting for speakers to finish and commenting on or questioning the previous speaker before making their own points.

Shared Writing

When the discussion began to focus on a particularly high-interest event, the teachers suggested that the group write an experience chart. As the children composed aloud, Zena recorded their thoughts on large chart paper. While encouraging all of the children to contribute in some way to the piece of shared writing, Zena recorded as precisely as possible what each child said. However, by carefully wording questions, she helped the children contribute appropriately to the overall shape or form of the writing. Zena then encouraged the children to build on the previously written sentences before

> At the zoo we saw lots of wild cats. They had caves to sleep in. The lions were playing games. They were jumping over each other. The tigers had stripes. They were running and play-fighting. Some were resting. The leopards had spots. They were walking around. They were beautiful.

> We saw monkeys at the zoo. They were playing. One monkey jumped and crashed into the gate. One monkey was throwing a piece of wood and cut his hand. He didn't even cry! We saw a spider monkey swinging with his tail.

making their own contributions. Before long, the various groups had composed stories, a recount of the trip, a letter, and a nonfiction informational piece. The various drafts were hung up on the wall.

The experience just described is called *shared writing* because the teacher and children composed the text together. The teachers helped children compose in different genres, rather than exclusively in a typical narrative or retelling mode.

For example, one group gave a general account of the day in a personal style, one told a story about the monkey's antics, and another related what they had learned about fur, feathers, and scales in a more direct, factual manner.

Later, Cheryl and Zena had their students match word cards to the words on the experience charts, work on sentence building exercises, and study other procedures for developing word and graphophonic knowledge. You can also use experience charts for word sorts according to visual patterns, letter clusters, or word groups—such as animal words, action words, and color words.

Modeling Spelling Behaviors

Zena and Cheryl allowed the children to see the process of spelling in action and occasionally *thought aloud* as the composing process progressed. For example, when a student dictated, "The monkey was called Mzuri," Cheryl acted and verbalized in the following way.

Action	Verbalization
Wrote "The monkey was called"	"Now, *Mzuri*. How am I going to spell that? I know it starts with a capital *m* because *Mzuri* is a name."
Wrote *M*.	"What can I hear next?" She said *Mzuri* once or twice, emphasizing the *s* sound.
Wrote *z*	She said *Mzuri* several more times and finally said, "It sounds like the word *zoo* in the middle! Maybe it's ..."
Wrote *oo*	"It's definitely *r* next."
Wrote *r*	"And I remember that it had an *i* on the end."

Wrote *i*   "I'm not quite sure about the *oo* in the middle. It doesn't look right. I'll just underline it so that we can come back to it later."

Underlined the *oo*

"Think alouds" like this, that go into details of spelling a word, should not occur too often, but the modeling of spelling strategies in this way is extremely valuable for young spellers. Those who are just starting to make graphophonic connections definitely benefit because this strategy shows them that it is legitimate to put down what they think is correct and continue to write.

Revising and Editing Their Work

In a later session, the teachers and their students returned to the first drafts of their experience charts. They obviously enjoyed rereading the texts. After discussing their initial reactions and responses, the children made suggestions for improvements, and the teachers implemented them. In such a situation, you would become a legitimate member of the group, and you could involve yourself in the discussion unobtrusively. You also could appropriately intervene by modeling revision strategies, such as adding text, moving text, and deleting text. In addition, you could suggest changes to vocabulary and sentence structure to make the writers' meaning clearer. By using text created by the children themselves, you would be much more confident about your students' engagement with tasks that focus on form, sequence, sentence structure, grammar, and graphophonic connections. With Zena and Cheryl's support, the children also edited the experience charts about the zoo trip for correct spelling. This was an opportunity for modeling have-a-go strategies. For example, with the children, they determined whether or not they should underline additional words for attention and applied have-a-go strategies by writing the words several different ways. If the students still weren't certain of the spelling of a word, a volunteer child found the word in the room or the teachers supplied it. Then they edited the charts for end punctuation, a skill the children had been using in their own writing. Finally, when their experience charts were the best they could be, the children took turns rewriting them so that other children could read them easily. The teachers found this to be a good opportunity to stress the importance of penmanship.

Publishing Their Work

Zena and Cheryl were then ready to have their students publish their revised and edited texts into individual books. Working together, the teachers and their students first decided where page breaks should go. During this activity, the teachers had several opportunities to focus their students' attention on sections or units of meaning within the overall text structure. As they were making their decisions, one student made an important observation when she said, "Those two sentences about furry animals should go together on one page." Another student added, "The words about traveling up on the bus and being excited could go together, and I will draw the bus." Once the children had determined the page breaks, Zena typed the text. Finally, the children cut the text apart, pasted the sentences into already stapled blank books, and illustrated their own copies.

Using Their Books

During a reading workshop, Zena and Cheryl's classes used both their individual books and the experience charts in all of the following ways.

1. They read to the children.

Cheryl and Zena always made a deliberate point to read the texts in ways appropriate for the forms and styles in which they had been written. For example, with great humor and excitement, they read the story about the orangutan that threw an orange at the children. They read the factual recount about the animals' fur, feathers, and scales like a nonfiction book, making references to the diagrams and illustrations.

2. Children read with their teachers.

When reading with the children, Cheryl and Zena often used the wall charts because they were big enough for everyone to see. The size also allowed the teachers to point out particular aspects of the text that they wanted their students to focus on. Sometimes they had choral readings, and the teachers discovered that even their least confident readers joined in from time to time. All of their students were able to participate in some way, and as they were reading and reviewing content, they were not only making valuable connections for phonics and spelling, but they were also tuning into such important areas as punctuation marks, vocabulary, the use of spaces, word usage, and fluency. In other words, during experiences such as these, their students were learning skills that applied to both reading and writing. Dean, an emergent reader, read the familiar charts with enthusiasm, though he mimicked reading when he came to a word or a section he was unsure of. Zena and Cheryl didn't assign him more drill work. Instead, they knew that as he was coming in and out of the reading of the text, he was learning important lessons about reading. For example, he was becoming more familiar with the text and picking up extra cues to aid his word identification. Dean was proud to be a part of the classroom reading community.

3. Children read by themselves.

After hearing the texts composed by the other groups and reading them with the teachers, many children were able to read them independently. Then Zena and Cheryl made the children's individual books from each of the groups available for independent reading both in school and at home. As the children read these books over

94

and over again, they reinforced sight vocabulary and the spelling of high use words and content words related to the unit on animals.

Following Up with Graphophonic Activities

Zena and Cheryl often have their students revisit the wall charts, over which they have hung clear plastic so that they and their students can mark words on the charts. When asked, the children are able to identify and circle words with certain letters or letter clusters, and they are able to identify and underline words with a particular sound, regardless of spelling.

After the children had several opportunities to focus on meaning, they played a game called "Let's Be Silly" (Jean Rachubinski, 1992) by reading the charts backwards. This game helped them recognize familiar words out of context and also helped them proofread. At other times, the teachers placed stick-on notes over some of the words for a cloze activity. Also, after duplicating the charts, they cut them into sentence strips, phrases, or words and then ask pairs of children to work together to reconstruct the whole text. During this activity, they allowed pairs to use the original chart as a reference.

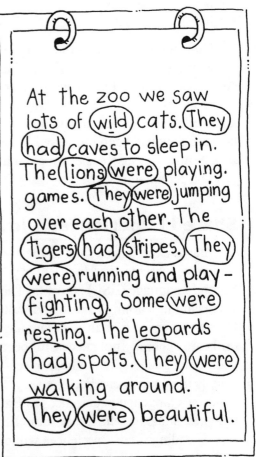

Writing Their Own Texts

Very soon after the excursion, several children were already working on their own pieces about the zoo during writing workshop. Cheryl and Zena actively encouraged others to write their own independent texts based on their zoo experiences by asking the following questions.

- What did you see in the reptile enclosure?
- How did it make you feel?
- What did you think of...?
- What happened when...?
- What would you do if...?

They negotiated with others to write something related to the broader integrated unit on animals that was being studied at that time. As a result of all of the preceding work and activities, the children's concepts and understandings about animals and zoos had grown, their knowledge had increased, and their vocabularies had broadened because they had been immersed in language about animals and the zoo. Now it was also easier for even the less confident writers to tackle a personal piece of writing.

Shared Experiences with ESL Students

Shared experiences such as the zoo trip that Zena and Cheryl's students experienced are particularly important for English as a Second Language (ESL) students. These children will be most successful in learning to read and write in English if they first share their experiences in their own language. Isolated phonics and spelling drills are generally not successful because many children who speak another language may not hear or recognize the sounds of English — sounds in isolation can become very distorted. Teachers rewrite children's language experiences in English and they share the English together. Students who know some English can dictate their understandings and experiences while the teacher takes dictation. As with emergent readers, the texts are read together over and over. It is also helpful to cut the text into strips and later into words for matching and rebuilding activities.

Highly predictable poems, rhymes, and songs that are shared as part of the science and social studies units are especially effective for ESL children to learn. Since they have experienced the content, the texts may have accompanying actions which help illustrate the words, and when they read these poems and songs over and over again, they can easily memorize them; therefore, they can focus on graphophonic features. The activities in Chapters 3, 4, and the beginning of this chapter are all appropriate for ESL children.

Shared Experiences with Older Students

Shared experiences like the zoo example should occur throughout all the grades. As children develop independent skills, they should more frequently do shared writing in cooperative groups with a "recorder" taking dictation. As a result, they will have an even greater need to spell correctly, and when they receive help from others in the group, they are more likely to remember words. Older students can use learning logs as a way to record data from research, reading, and firsthand experiences. If they keep their learning logs with them while they are on field trips, as they plan projects, and when they collect data, they can use them to reflect on their learning and record generalizations about what they know. Eventually, writing should become a natural way to think. Keep in mind, however, that because these writers are writing mostly for themselves, they may not attend to the spelling in their logs as much as in more polished drafts, but you will most assuredly see a change in their spelling when their writing is going to have an audience.

Recording, Evaluating, and Reporting

As teachers shift their teaching strategies toward whole language, many will naturally wonder from time to time if their students are learning to read and spell in their new whole language classrooms as well as they might have with more traditional teaching methods. Most teachers would agree that it's not easy to let go of past practices like workbooks and weekly spelling tests and still feel confident that they're teaching effectively. The evaluation tools and strategies discussed in Chapter 6 will help to assure you that your students are learning all of the important skills and that the risks you seem to be taking in your teaching methods are, indeed, worth taking. Student evaluation is not only a means to help teachers understand what their students know and still need to learn, but it is also an essential means of keeping parents informed. Whole language teachers usually must do more than make routine progress reports to parents. They also help parents better understand the goals of their whole language programs and how their children are actually learning phonics and spelling. Chapter 7, therefore, will help you answer some of the difficult questions parents often ask and show you ways to involve parents so that they can experience firsthand what their children are learning.

Chapter 6

Recording and Evaluating

Since whole language teachers teach skills in the context of meaningful reading and writing, it only makes sense to evaluate those skills in the same way. In fact, your students should rarely be able to tell the difference between learning and evaluation activities.

An important part of any ongoing evaluation process is gathering data. Every time you observe your students—listening to them read or reviewing their writing samples and other artifacts (such as logs, audio-tapes, or journals)—you are actually gathering important data. How you use this data depends in large measure on exactly what you're evaluating, why you're evaluating it, and for whom you're evaluating it. Although this chapter is about recording and evaluating graphophonic understandings specifically, you may find it useful to generalize the strategies to your entire language program.

Evaluating Skills in Context

Keeping the complexity of reading and writing in mind, you can often understand what your students know about phonics and spelling by examining their miscues—variations from the text or nonconventional spellings—that they make during their reading and writing. By studying these miscues, you will be able to identify the various patterns of children's graphophonic knowledge.

As we stated in the introduction to this section, graphophonic relationships are best examined through patterns of use in natural reading and writing contexts where you can analyze spelling and phonics from a developmental perspective, instead of from a single standard of correctness. By understanding the three stages of spelling/phonic development that are outlined on the following chart, you can use your students' miscues and temporary spellings as indicators of their progress along a developmental continuum. Of course, because the indicators represent a continuum, children may demonstrate characteristics of more than one stage at any given time.

EMERGENT (prephonetic)

Writing and Reading:

- Develops a knowledge of the alphabet.

- Develops a conceptualization that print carries messages.

- Understands that numbers and other letter-like symbols may be part of writing.

- Develops a conceptualization that letters have sounds and words can be represented with letters. (Words may be represented with one, two, or three letters—often matching the letter names rather than sounds; such as *cd* = *seed* and *left* = *elephant*.)

- Develops a knowledge of left-to-right directionality with the return sweep. (A child may begin at left but continue a word or line of print from right to left.)

continued

---

continued

- May mix upper- and lowercase letters in writing. (This same skill may be only partially recognized in reading.)

- Use of spaces between words may not be evident in writing; may not have one-to-one match when pointing to words being read to the child.

NOVICE (phonetic or transitional*)

Writing:

- Represents all or most of the sounds in words with letters, but may still confuse vowel sounds.

- Uses many conventional spellings.

- Uses word segmentation and directionality appropriately.

- Uses both vowels and consonants; vowels begin to appear in each syllable.

- Uses both sight and sound spelling strategies. (For example, *have* is spelled *hava* because the child knows the word is four letters long.)

- Uses some inflectional endings such as *-ed, -s,* and *-ing*.

Reading:

- Develops a one-to-one match between speech and print.

- Recognizes commonly used sight words.

- "Reads" a predictable text fluently after hearing the words once or twice.

- Makes meaningful substitutions when reading.

- Develops the use of picture clues and all three cue systems for decoding unknown words.

continued

continued

INDEPENDENT (fluent*)

Writing:

• Understands basic knowledge of spelling patterns.

• Understands knowledge of word structure, including affixes, contractions, and compound words.

• Continues to master vowel patterns, double consonant patterns, silent consonants, and other spelling patterns.

• Continues to master irregular spellings.

• Develops a large accumulation of conventional spellings.

Reading:

• Self-corrects by rereading to make sense.

• Reads silently and takes risks with new materials.

• Reads fluently, making predictions using all available cues.

• Knows most phonic generalizations and can decode words, even in isolation.

*Based on spelling stages identified by Henderson & Beers (1980) and Gentry (1982).

Collecting, Recording, and Analyzing Information

What information you collect, how you collect it, and how you record it depends on your students' various stages of literacy development and your own personal management system. There are, some common methods for collecting and recording information and artifacts during the reading and writing processes. Although each of these methods takes more time than a single test, you should keep in mind that you will be constructing emerging collages of your students over a period of time. The multiple contexts in which you collect your information will also make these collages rich and informative, rather than just the quick snapshot a test provides. If at first you find evaluating in context over time difficult, remind yourself that change is an evolutionary process. It's important that you feel confident that you:

- **understand how** to promote the conditions for effective learning of reading, writing, and spelling;

- **know the major reading** and spelling strategies and how to help children use them;

- **have a growing knowledge** of the major checkpoints of language development for each child in your class;

- **have consistent theories** of reading, writing, phonics and spelling in order to develop an integrated program in which all aspects of language learning support each other.

If you are just emerging into whole language, we suggest that you proceed with caution with your evaluation until you feel comfortable that you have sufficient support and resources. Administrators need to provide time and adequate professional development when helping teachers to implement new evaluation procedures for phonics or spelling.

At this point, it's important to note that you will not have to collect detailed information on every student for every aspect of their learning. You likely know what most of your students know and don't know—you have collected a lot of data. How do you now analyze that data to determine specific strengths and needs that can lead to improved learning? The following evaluation strategies should help you to gather and analyze data about your students and then help you to see patterns that provide evidence of their effective strategies as well as their needs. However, you will have to decide which of these evaluations tools you think will work best for you.

Classroom Observations

Teachers have always observed students and made decisions based on those observations, but in 1980, Yetta Goodman legitimized kid-watching as an effective evaluation tool. In fact, information gained from observation may be the most valid data you can gather about the processes and strategies children use to learn.

Observation as an Evaluation Tool

A first grader was writing a story about a trip to the pumpkin patch. After she wrote *Pmp*, she sounded out the phoneme /k/, but she wasn't certain how to make the letter *k*. She left her seat momentarily, looked up at the alphabet chart above the chalkboard, and then began to quietly sing the "The ABC Song." As she pointed toward the letters, her one-to-one correspondence must have been off slightly because when she returned to her seat she wrote *j*. When the teacher read her finished product *pmpjn*, she was puzzled by the unusual spelling. It is only by observing the process by which students learn that a teacher would have seen that the girl knew the sound and the corresponding letter name, but she just didn't know how to form the letter.

All teachers can become good observers if they make time for careful observations, understand the reading and writing processes, and know what they want their students to achieve. In addition, the teachers who are the most effective kid-watchers are those who allow their students to be independent learners. Of course, it's not always easy to stand back and observe without intervening. This becomes easier, however, when you keep your observations as unobtrusive as possible by standing back at a distance or by pulling your chair away slightly from the group. These little physical separations can help you better observe how your students learn from each other and how they seek information from the available texts and resources in your room.

Observation should be a part of your regular schedule. We believe that you can actually *plan* who you will observe, so that even in a very large class, you should be able to make time for significant observations of each student. You should, however, be prepared to take advantage of unexpected events that can reveal important information about your students and what they know.

Anecdotal Records

Different teachers develop different ways to record observations of their students' progress in reading and spelling. For example, some jot down brief narratives on index cards, and others write quick notes on a clipboard that includes a page for each of their students. As you observe, note incidents that will tell you about your learners' strategies, concepts of literacy, and attitudes.

Observation Checklists

Teachers who find anecdotal records unwieldy sometimes create checklists such as the following sample checklist to accomplish the same goals. Designed to capture frequency of specific literacy behaviors over time, these checklists should reflect the critical components of a language arts curriculum.

Checklists that include space for anecdotal notes are also common. Remember that when observing graphophonic skills, it's as important to note a student's overuse of certain cues as it is to note their lack of use. Using phrases such as not apparent at this time and inconsistent use indicate that phonics and spelling are developmental. This form of evaluation eliminates the false perception that these skills are mastered once and for all.

SAMPLE CHECKLIST FOR GRAPHOPHONIC
CUES IN READING AND WRITING

NA=Not apparent at this time I=Inconsistently E=Efficiently OU=Overused

NAME _____

Date:						
• Recognizes initial sounds						
• Recognizes the dominant sound in a word						
• Analyzes words into sound segments						
• Writes letters or letter clusters to represent initial or dominant sounds						
• Writes letters or letter clusters to represent all the sound segments						
• Recognizes rhyming sounds						
• Uses graphophonic knowledge to check predictions while reading						
• Uses graphophonic knowledge to self-correct reading miscues						
• Uses graphophonic knowledge to self-correct spelling miscues						
• Uses effective strategies for decoding unfamiliar words						
• Uses effective strategies for spelling unfamiliar words						

Interviews, Conversations, and Conferences

If you want to know how children are progressing, just ask them! During conferences, even very young children can describe the strategies they use when reading and writing. The following questions can help guide your conversations, interviews, and conferences, related to decoding and spelling. At the same time, you can easily assess your students' attitudes toward words and spelling.

Decoding

- When you're reading and you come to a word you don't know, what do you do?
- Do you ever do anything else?
- Whom would you ask for help in reading? Why do you ask that person?
- Do you ever skip a word when you're reading? Tell me more about what you do.
- Why do you sometimes stop yourself and go back and reread?
- Are you a good reader? Why do you think so?

Adapted from Carolyn Burke's Reading Inventory (Burke, 1979).

Spelling

- What do you do when you think you don't know how to spell a word?
- What else could you do?
- Whom do you ask for help with spelling? Why do you ask that person?
- How do you look for a word in the dictionary?
- Where else could you look to find the spelling of a word?
- How do you know if the spelling of a word is correct?
- What makes you decide to change the spelling of a word?
- Are you a good speller? Why do you think so?

Adapted from Barmby & Jones, 1991.

Interviews, conversations, and conferences provide you with valuable evaluative information, but they also provide your students with insights into their own thinking, help them to clarify the strategies they use, and help them develop a "decoding and spelling conscience." It is only when children become aware of their own strengths and weaknesses that they can begin to set goals for their own learning. Conferences and conversations between or among students can be just as useful as those between you and your students. Listening to student-to-student conferences can provide you with insights into both students' understandings.

Global Writing Assessments

You can focus your evaluation on your students' written products as well as on the strategies they used during writing. For example, you could use the following writing sample, "A Cricket and Basketball," and the global assessment form on page 110 to record a global assessment for writing. You can develop a similar global assessment form for reading. These forms may be completed for four or five students each month, but all of the children in your class should have at least one global assessments during the year.

> (cricket)
> I play cricket for plenty.
> Last Saturday we played
> Greensbough. I have to go to
> bed at 11:30 at night
> Last Saturday we won
> by 17 runs. ~~/////~~ against
> Greensbough. ~~to start playing Basketball~~ I am going
> ~~now team anyway.~~
> I am going to keep playing
> basketball now.
>   On Saturday we play
> Dimond creek. On Friday
> night we play st ~~Kames~~
> (fomerser's). Then I wil go
> home and play with Ryan,
> and my other friends.
>   The
>   end

Name: *Paul H.* Grade: *1* Text: *Cricket & Basketball* Date: *July 22*

Meaning	Organization	Language	Spelling	Mechanics
Subject matter/Field Ideas Topic knowledge Presentation of information	Form/Genre Structure Focus/Sequence/ Links Readers' needs	Grammar/Usage/ Sentence structure Vocabulary Style/Mood Voice	Graphophonic connections Visual memory Morphemic knowledge Helping Strategies/ Independence	Handwriting/Features of print Punctuation Layout/Graphic features Word processing
Subject matter is clear; Paul is writing about his "passion in life." Sense of ownership is strong. Information given about team, and when it plays.	Written in personal recount genre. Text organization appropriate. - orientation (telling who, what and when) - series of events - some personal comments. Good sequencing (Exception-sentence 3 seems thrown in).	Language appropriate at Grade 1. Language features relevant to genre: - 1st person pronouns - specific participants - mainly simple past tense - time links ("Last Saturday...", "On Friday...") Flowing easy to read style. Strong sense of "voice."	Paul's spelling is at a stage beyond what could be expected halfway through Grade 1. He feels free to "have a go." He circled a word to check, but didn't proceed to a written form of publication. However punctuation was appropriate.	This piece was published by recording it on tape for others to listen to: The "mechanics" of writing are assessed on <u>final</u> product.

Comments (Observed needs/Future challenges/Teaching points)
Perhaps Paul is unsure about focus. This could be two pieces - one about cricket and the other about basketball. Needs to give more thought to titles.

Adapted from Brown & Mathie (1990)

Self-Evaluations

From the very beginning of their schooling, children should be encouraged to evaluate their own work and to participate in setting goals for their own learning. Therefore, you can use any of the following procedures to help your students conduct self-evaluations.

SELF-EVALUATION PROCEDURES

1. **Have your students tape themselves as they read,** then evaluate their rendition of the text as they listen to the tape. This method of self-evaluation is especially good for children who need work on fluency or for those whose fluency and comprehension are good but who miscue frequently due to insufficient attention to graphophonic cues.

2. **Have your students keep literature and/or learning logs.** In addition to having your students write their own summaries and reflections about what they have read, you also might want them to keep lists of unknown or interesting vocabulary words, which they should define according to how they are used in context.

3. **Have your students self-assess misspellings by circling words or parts of words during revision or editing of any written work that will be published.** This method also allows you to observe what your students know about spelling.

4. **Encourage students to ask themselves the same kinds of questions that you have asked them during reading and writing conferences.** In writing conferences, for example, they could ask the following questions to draw attention to spelling.

   • Does that word look right?

   • Are there any letters missing in this word?

   • Where would the missing letters go?

   • Can I find any other words that I think need checking or are misspelled?

continued

continued

In reading conferences, they could ask the following questions.

- Did that word make sense?

- Does it begin with the same letter?

5. **Have your students keep checklists and other open-ended forms that help them with self-evaluation.** Some teachers use the rating forms on pages 113-116 for self-evaluation of spelling and reading with children from second grade up.

6. **Encourage your students to write about their own strategies for decoding, building vocabulary, and spelling**. For example, you may want to try a few of the following strategies and then add some of your own.

- Words I want to learn to spell.

- Words I know and how I remember them.

- Interesting and unusual words.

- What I've learned about spelling that helps me in my reading.

- What I've learned in my reading that helps me in my spelling.

- Strategies I use when I don't know how to read a word.

- Strategies I use when I don't know how to spell a word.

AM I BECOMING A GOOD SPELLER?

Name: _____ **Grade:** _____

	DATE	LOW	←		→	HIGH
I care about spelling. I want to be a good speller. I know that correct spelling is important when I write for others.						
I write often. The more I write, the more I am practicing spelling. I may not stop to check a spelling as I write my first draft, but I always check when I revise the draft.						
I proofread my writing. I finally proofread any writing I will pass to readers. In doing this, I inspect every word and all punctuation. Sometimes I also get a partner to check my proofing.						
I read every day. Reading leaves impressions of spelling in my mind. It also adds to the number of words I use. While reading, I sometimes pause to notice spellings.						
I practice legible handwriting. My spacing and formation of letters affects my spelling. I take care with my handwriting and proofread my writing for legibility.						

Name: _____ **Grade:** _____

	DATE	LOW ←——————→ HIGH				

I explore words.

For example, I notice letter-patterns like *tion, ough,* and *qu,* and prefixes (like *dis-*) and suffixes (like *-less*). I also notice meaning stems, as in *paragraph, biography,* and *telegraphic.*

I check to be sure.

Sometimes while writing, I ask for the spelling of a word, but I know that the final way to settle a doubt about a spelling is to consult a dictionary.

I learn new spellings.

1. I look at a new word and say it softly.
2. I cover it and try to "see" it in my mind.
3. I write it from memory.
4. I check (and if incorrect, repeat the four steps).

TEACHER COMMENTS:

AM I BECOMING A GOOD READER?

Name: _____   **Grade:** _____

	DATE	LOW ← → HIGH			

I read often. I read independently.

I enjoy reading quietly. I enjoy the daily reading time. I choose to read at other times during the day. I choose to read at home. I know what to do when I don't understand something or know a word. I choose varied materials. I choose materials at the right level for independent reading.

I am a word watcher.

I am interested in new words. I try to figure out new words using all the strategies I know. I try to learn what new words mean. I try to use the interesting words I read in my writing and my speech. I like to study words to learn their sounds, their roots, and any related words.

I take part in conferences.

I prepare for the conference. I speak freely with the teacher and the group. I talk about what I think the author means. I listen to what others say. I try to understand what others say and respond to that.

I respond to reading.

I keep my Reading Log up-to-date. I share my Reading Log with others. I complete a variety of activities. The activities I choose are appropriate to what I have read. I look for other books by my favorite authors.

Name: _____ **Grade:** _____

	DATE	LOW	←	→	HIGH

I read in social studies and science.

I use nonfiction books when necessary. I understand how to read graphs, charts, maps, etc. I know how to use reference books like encyclopedias and an atlas. I choose nonfiction for interest.

I share my reading.

I prepare for share time. I consider the audience. My confidence has improved. I am willing to share with others. I help others find out about books.

TEACHER COMMENTS:

Examining Miscues in Reading and Spelling

To help you learn about the processes your students may be using when reading and writing, you could study writing samples, audiotapes of them reading, and/or running records of their oral reading. By examining artifacts such as these, you can make evaluation more meaningful for parents and students and make important comparisons over time. To be most effective during evaluation, every piece of writing a child produces should be dated and stored in writing folders. (Hanging file folders for each child will help you quickly distribute writing folders each day and will make it easier for parents, teachers, or other concerned parties to quickly review them.) Audiotapes and other documentation, such as running records, should also be dated and stored. By following these simple procedures, you will be able to follow your students' general progress in reading and writing over time, as well as note specific progress in spelling and decoding.

When you analyze data at any one point in time—or over a period of time—you should look for patterns in spelling and reading miscues that can provide you with insight into the various strategies your students are using correctly, overusing, or not using at all. (Rather than viewing students' variations from the text as errors, we prefer to use the term *miscues*.) The first question you should always ask yourself is, Is the reader/writer trying to make sense? Next, look for patterns of self-correction. Then examine common miscue patterns in both reading and spelling to better understand what strategies need to be taught. Some common miscue patterns include the following.

MISCUE PATTERNS

- **Substitutions of letters, letter clusters, or entire words** (for example, in writing: *sed* for *said*; in reading: /sade/ for *said*)

- **Omissions of letters, letter clusters, or entire words** (for example, in writing: *movd* for *moved*; in reading: *move* for *moved*)

- **Insertions of letters, letter clusters, or entire words** (for example, in writing: *disscussion* for *discussion*; in reading: *the children* for *children*)

- **Transpositions of letters or letter clusters** (for example, in writing: *recieve* for *receive*; in reading: *saw* for *was*)

- **Differences in dialect** (for example, in writing: *rewn* for *ruin*; in reading: *stop* for *stopped*)

- **Faulty auditory perceptions** (for example, in writing: *quacker* for *cracker*; in reading: *white* for right)

Reading Miscues and Running Records

Keeping running records of reading behaviors during oral reading of unfamiliar material—or in some cases during oral readings of familiar text—can help you gain insights into the strategies your students use to construct meaning as they read. Although this recording method is simple to use and doesn't require special forms, it does require some practice because you systematically need to observe what strategies your readers are using to construct meaning—not just what words they can't read. We suggest the following combination of ideas from Marie Clay's *The Early Detection of Reading Difficulties* (1979) and Yetta Goodman, Dorothy Watson, and Carolyn Burke's *Reading Miscue Inventory* (1989). Record the miscues a reader makes during oral reading of a text so that you can analyze them later. Self-corrections of any of the miscues previously listed usually indicates that a reader is trying to construct meaning; however, other miscues may also indicate that the same reader is constructing meaning from the text. A reader can read a sentence from the text with several miscues, not self-correct, and still not change the meaning of the text significantly. Try this with the sentence you just read.

Readers

"A reader can read a sentence from the text with several

miscues, not self correct, and still not change the meaning of the text

significantly.

✓ = read correctly
A, can = omissions
Reader, not, not = substitution

Even though the verb tense and the number of subjects changed in this sentence, the meaning did not. The reader ignored the initial graphophonic cues in two words, but you could still feel fairly certain that he or she knows letter-sound correspondence. If one of your students had made the above miscues, he would still be considered an effective reader because the sentence made sense semantically and syntactically. When analyzing reading strategies, compare each miscue to the printed text. Miscues can be classified as similar in meaning (semantics), grammar (syntax), or visual/phonetic (graphophonic) cues. The following chart summarizes a simple form of miscue analysis, including retelling.

RECORDING MISCUES

You can record the miscues on a blank sheet of paper. All the various miscues are demonstrated in the following sentence:

Spiders often have many eyes so that they can see their prey.

Omission: ✓ ✓ ✓ ✓ ✓ ✓ ✓ ✓ ✓ ✓ ✓

Substitution: ✓ ✓ ✓ ✓ ✓ ✓ ✓ ✓ ✓ ✓ ✓ prée / prey

Insertion: ✓ ✓ ✓ too ✓ ✓ ✓ ✓ ✓ ✓ ✓ ✓

Reversal / inversion: Spiders often ✓ ✓ ✓ ✓ ✓ ✓ ✓ ✓ ✓

Repetition: R ⌐ Spiders often have ┘ ✓ ✓ ✓ ✓ ✓ ✓ ✓ ✓ ✓

Self-Correction: ✓ ✓ ✓ ✓ ✓ ✓ ✓ ✓ ✓ ✓ ✓ ©prée / prey

ANALYZING MISCUES

The analysis of running records, according to Marie Clay's method, is quantitative with some regard to the quality of the miscues that were self-corrected. We recommend the reading miscue inventory approach instead. This is a qualitative analysis. Thus, we do not intend to use this method for finding instructional reading levels or placement in materials. What is important is not the number of errors, but instead the patterns of miscues. These will provide valuable information about the reader's strategies.

To better understand this concept, reexamine the miscues explained above. Each reader miscue is analyzed to compare similarity with the original text. Miscues are rated as similar (Y), not similar (N), and partially similar (P).

SEMANTIC	SYNTACTIC	GRAPHOPHONIC	MEANING CHANGE
Y N P	Y N P	Y N P	Y N P

Then evaluate the reader's strategies by asking the following questions and studying patterns.

continued

continued

- Is constructing meaning the central strategy?

- Is the author's intended meaning changed?*

- Is the reader overusing graphophonic cues to the exclusion of semantic and syntactic cues?

- Is the reader confused about graphophonic cues?

- Is faulty articulation, dialect, or faulty auditory perception causing miscues?

*Each time a reader reads, she creates personal meaning for the text. Likewise, it is difficult to fully determine an author's intended meaning. The intent here is to examine match of meaning between author and reader as closely as possible.

ANALYZING RETELLINGS

The reader is asked to retell what he read. The retelling analysis should reinforce or better explain the analysis of miscues.

For students whom you're particularly concerned about, you'll want to take running records regularly—perhaps weekly if you're puzzled by a child's behavior, but less often as things improve. By analyzing miscues and having the child retell what he or she has read, you'll be able to determine which strategies to emphasize and which to de-emphasize. Ineffective readers generally overuse graphophonic cues and don't attend to meaning.

Some teachers also find it useful to prepare running record forms for entire texts that are used frequently in their teaching program (as in the sample, these texts may be 10 to 20 pages long). These teachers usually make multiple copies of these forms so that they are available for immediate use. As you can see on the sample running record form on page 123, the text is double-spaced, and it includes three columns to record the miscues, the self-corrections, and the analysis of the miscues.

Spelling Miscues

By collecting and analyzing the spelling miscues that your students make, you will be able to gain insights into what information about spelling they are or are not applying, and those insights will lead you to the discovery of children's patterns of language behavior. Then you can use this information to assist children with specific strategies. Bean & Bouffler (1987, p. 85) suggest that you ask yourself the following questions to help you better understand prevalent patterns of behavior.

- Is the writer able to produce spellings that serve the purpose of recording meaning? To do this, the spellings have to be sufficiently systematic for meaning to be retrieved over time. Does the writer have sufficient spelling strategies to allow this?

- Does spelling interfere with the process of writing? In other words, does a concern for spelling restrict a writer's composing?

- Does the writer understand the demands of proofreading, as opposed to reading? Is the writer able to recognize nonstandard forms?

- Having recognized nonstandard spelling, is the writer able to standardize it? If this involves recourse to a dictionary, does the writer have the alphabetic knowledge required to use one? Is the writer able to produce likely alternative spellings for a word?

By keeping these questions in mind, you will be able to focus on "spelling as meaning," and everyone would agree that spelling is best learned when the words mean something and when they are used for authentic communication. A good idea is to collect spelling miscues

122

Level 2   **SOUP**

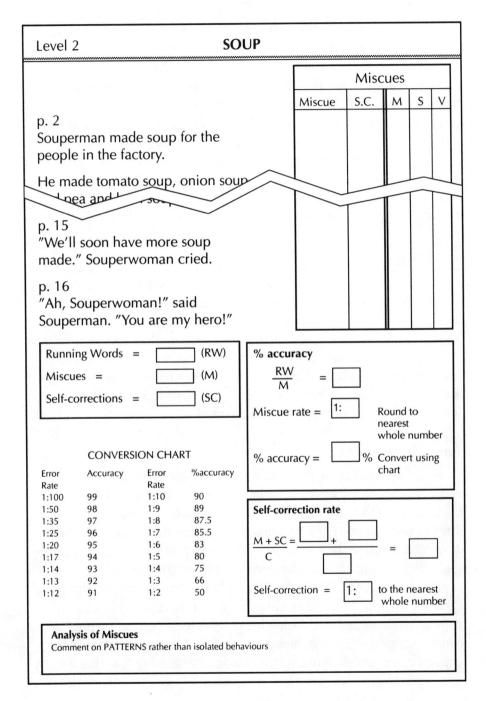

Miscues				
Miscue	S.C.	M	S	V

p. 2
Souperman made soup for the
people in the factory.

He made tomato soup, onion soup

p. 15
"We'll soon have more soup
made." Souperwoman cried.

p. 16
"Ah, Souperwoman!" said
Souperman. "You are my hero!"

Running Words = [   ] (RW)

Miscues = [   ] (M)

Self-corrections = [   ] (SC)

% accuracy

$$\frac{RW}{M} = \boxed{}$$

Miscue rate = 1:[ ]   Round to nearest whole number

% accuracy = [ ] % Convert using chart

CONVERSION CHART

Error Rate	Accuracy	Error Rate	%accuracy
1:100	99	1:10	90
1:50	98	1:9	89
1:35	97	1:8	87.5
1:25	96	1:7	85.5
1:20	95	1:6	83
1:17	94	1:5	80
1:14	93	1:4	75
1:13	92	1:3	66
1:12	91	1:2	50

Self-correction rate

$$\frac{M + SC}{C} = \frac{\boxed{} + \boxed{}}{\boxed{}} = \boxed{}$$

Self-correction = 1:[ ] to the nearest whole number

Analysis of Miscues
Comment on PATTERNS rather than isolated behaviours

from various samples of your students' writing over time so that you will be able to discover basic, representative patterns. Then, in order to analyze the spelling miscues you've recorded, group them into categories. As you begin to categorize them on a chart—such as the example on page 125—focus your attention on overall spelling miscues—rather than just on individual ones. If you do this, you probably will find that the major areas of weakness will cluster in certain broad categories. Remember, you will only need to closely analyze spelling miscues for children who are having difficulty, but being trained to do this alters the way in which you will perceive and interpret all your students' spelling miscues.

Testing

A single test, such as a standardized test, causes teachers, students, and parents to view phonics and spelling as products because all of the test items are scored as either right or wrong. But if reading and writing are for meaning, you should be assessing the process as well as the product. For example, even if you administer a standard spelling test, you can place less emphasis on the score and concentrate more on assessing spelling patterns; thus drawing conclusions about the spelling strategies your students likely used.

The Cloze Procedure

In an informal cloze procedure, your students will fill in blanks left in the text, using whatever knowledge and experience they have. Later, as you talk with them about their predictions, you will help them to become aware of the reading strategies they used and how to develop and refine their strategies. This procedure also allows you to study their graphophonic knowledge as part of their decoding strategies. You can prepare the cloze text in various ways so that your students will use different reading skills and strategies. For example, you can evaluate semantic knowledge by deleting content words: nouns (not proper nouns), pronouns, verbs, adjectives, and adverbs. Or, you can evaluate syntactic knowledge by deleting function words,

SPELLING ANALYSIS

Word	Spelling	Phonic alternatives — Reasonable alternatives (including homophones)	Phonic alternatives — Alternatives not conforming to spelling precedent	Faulty auditory perception	Analysis of structure — Letters omitted	Letters added	Letters transposed	Letters substituted (c=consonant v=vowel)	Doubling errors	Similar visual configuration	Unclassifiable
creek	creek	✓						✓			
house	hows	✓						✓			
went	whent	✓									
lived	livde						✓				
nearly	nily				✓						
bitten	biten			Perhaps	✓						
great	grate	✓ homophone like "a" car						✓		✓	
stuck	stak	✓			✓			✓		✓	
swamp	swomp	✓						✓			
broke	browk	✓ homophone sounded out			✓			✓		✓	
piece	peace	✓						✓			
parade	prayed		✓					✓			
home	howm	✓	✓					✓			
again	agen	✓						✓		✓	
sign	cyn							c,v			

such as: conjunctions, prepositions, auxiliary verbs, and noun determiners. You can also evaluate your students' graphophonic connections by deleting letters and letter clusters. For example, you might ask yourself the following questions: Are my students reading for and developing meaning in order to make predictions about the missing letters and letter clusters? Are they using syntax (grammar) to help them make predictions? (For more detailed information about testing graphophonic connections, see Chapters 2 and 8 in Hornsby, Parry & Sukana, 1993.)

Spelling Lists and the Weekly Spelling Test

Your students can compile personal spelling lists from various sources such as their have-a-go cards. You can supplement these personal lists with words from the content of current units of work in social studies, science, and literature, as well as from high-frequency words, or "spelling demons." When you test your students on words from sources such as these, you will be moving spelling assessment away from "spelling as product" and towards "spelling as meaning" because the words on the tests directly relate to your classroom activities, whereas traditional weekly spelling tests take words from a published list that are unrelated in any way to the language and learning contexts in your classroom. When the words on your spelling tests have a connection to your students' lives, they not only will test your students in a meaningful way, but they will also provide the information that parents want and that you need.

Malcolm Hobbs
My Spelling List

Snake   cactus
reptile   weather
diamond humid
slither
vision
canyon

Weekly Spelling Tests

In Cathy Lasell's multi-age fourth/fifth-grade classroom, the children select spelling words from their own writing lists of high-frequency words and content words. Each child keeps his or her words in a spelling notebook. The children list 15 words they need to learn to spell. They also carry over words they didn't learn to spell during the previous test. Cathy gives them considerable guidance during the first few months of school and frequently models how to select words that are at their level of spelling ability. She helps students examine their own writing to determine which words are frequently misspelled and then encourages them to add these to their lists. She also helps them to select words from word lists. She teaches her children that they rarely use words in their writing that they do not use comfortably in their speaking vocabularies.

Over several days, the children compile their lists and study the words with their spelling partners. Partners, who should be at equal ability levels, check the words for immediate feedback. Then Cathy checks them as well, to assure accuracy. Then her students restudy their misspelled words and are later retested. When the children in Cathy's class check one anothers' papers, they circle the letters or letter clusters within a word that need work. Because these children have responsibility for their own learning, they take pride in their spelling and help one another with strategies for improvement.

Dictation

Traditional uses of dictation have not always proved valuable. However, if passages are linked to current classroom work that includes words taken from that work, contexts for "spelling as meaning" are extended. As with other forms of spelling assessment, the focus is then on monitoring development from temporary to conventionally correct spellings.

To use this procedure, dictate to individuals or small groups a short passage appropriate to your students' experiences. After dictating phrase by phrase, including punctuation, allow time for your students to proofread their spelling. You can analyze children's ability to recognize misspelled words and their strategies for corrections. You can also analyze these transcriptions for graphophonic understandings, but you will need to keep in mind what Clay (1979, 1991) has emphasized: It is important to study children's miscues at the phoneme and grapheme level, rather than at the word level. The following example dictated to a 7-year-old indicates the dramatic difference in the end result when you attend to graphophonic connections rather than checking words as either right or wrong.

Consider this sentence from a passage dictated to a 7-year-old:

```
 1    2    3 4 5  6  789   10  11 12 13  14 15 16 17 18  19  20 21 22 23  24  25  26  27 28 29 30 31  32 33 34
There  was  a  fireworks  display  after  the  football  game.
```

```
Thir  wus  a  friwerks  daseplay  after  the  football  game.
 ✓  ✗   ✓  ✗ ✓  ✓  ✓ ✗ ✗ ✓   ✗  ✓ ✓   ✓ ✗ ✓    ✓ ✓  ✓   ✓ ✓ ✓  ✓    ✓  ✓ ✓  ✓  ✓ ✓ ✓ ✓   ✓   ✓ ✓ ✓
```

Comparison of scoring at word level or graphophonic level

Word level score: 4/9 = 45%
Graphophonic connections: 28/34 = 85%

Standardized Tests

Many schools in the United States use formal, standardized tests for summative evaluation; however, these tests are most effective for program evaluation rather than individual assessment. If standardized tests are used, they are only one small piece of a very complex picture of the whole child.

Children who have been taught in whole language classrooms may be effective readers and spellers in everyday reading and writing situations, but many may be less effective when faced with the decontextualized format of a standardized test. For example, when children read a picture book, they use all the semantic cues (including the pictures), as well as syntactic and graphophonic cues, to decode words. On a standardized test, those same children are faced with tasks that require attendance to words in isolation. Stripped of all contextual clues, reading certain words becomes a more difficult task for all children—for students from whole language classrooms (who rarely, if ever, read words in isolation), this is simply *not* reading.

The directions used in standardized tests may be an even bigger handicap for children in whole language classrooms. However, you can prepare your students for these unfamiliar formats and tasks by providing them with practice exercises in the same formats that are included on standardized tests. This is not "teaching the test," it is helping your students become testwise. If you are ever on a selection committee for standardized tests, you should ask yourself the following questions.

- Does the format allow graphophonic skills to be tested in realistic reading and writing contexts?

- What is the purpose of using the test?

- Who is the audience?

- Is the test valid? (Does it measure what it is supposed to measure? Does it measure what students are supposed to be learning?)

- Is the group you're going to test comparable to the norm group?

- What will the test tell you that you don't already know or can't find out in other ways?

- How will the results be explained to the audience?

If you cannot find satisfactory answers to these questions, then you should question the validity of the test. Standardized tests do have a valid use. The Australian Council for Educational Research develops standardized tests which are given to a sample of, say, third graders across the country. Three or five years later, the same tests (or statistically equivalent versions) are given to another sample of third graders. The results are then used to make valuable statements about trends over time for third-grade students. With this approach, it would not even be necessary to write the children's names on the tests. It would be enough to simply identify the type of school and its community (urban/rural, socioeconomic level, ethnic composition, and so on.)

Test scores for individual children can never tell you what to do the next day to help those children—how can a stanine or a percentile help you to plan teaching strategies? For example, if the words below were on a standardized spelling test, the test scores for the following two children would be exactly the same. Clearly, however, the two children who wrote these words are not equivalent spellers, and they need different help from their teacher.

CHILD A	CHILD B
cat	cat
dog	dog
elefant	eluft
girarf	jrf
zeebra	zbru
Score: 2/5	2/5

Checkpoints

Although assessment data is gathered from *daily* reading and writing experiences, checkpoints throughout the school year can help you bring together, analyze, and record much of your assessment data and can help you provide a composite picture of each child's development. For example, the checkpoints in the Appendix on pages 156-161 can help give you confidence in your ongoing evaluation. These global assessments may be done for just four or five children each month, but all children in the class will have at least one global assessment during the year.

You may want to devise informal tests, analyze reading and spelling miscues, or conduct interviews periodically throughout the year to "triangulate" or add to the data already collected for these checkpoints through ongoing evaluation. These checkpoints are useless without the rich, ongoing data collected during reading and writing. As in all evaluation instruments, the checkpoints included below will need to be adapted to your particular classroom.

Evaluation in Perspective

You will want to keep the evaluation of phonics and spelling in perspective within the bigger picture of language and learning. Your evaluation also should *contribute* to learning, not *distract* from it. Your evaluation should be ongoing, since most effective teaching strategies provide multiple contexts for assessment. Remember, because you are a participant in the classroom, you will know more about what your students know than any test could ever tell. Therefore, you should rely on your professional knowledge and then learn ways to record this knowledge so that others will be able to recognize your students' knowledge and skills. The sample assessment overview for writing on page 132 shows the various assessment contexts and strategies that you can integrate into a yearly plan. You may want to devise a similar framework to use as part of your own yearly assessment plan for reading and writing.

Finally, it is difficult for teachers to actively participate in "teaching" while actively observing and making decisions about what needs to be learned next. Your role is to know how to set up the learning situation for necessary learning to occur. This means that the idea of "teacher" changes from "provider of information" to "facilitator of learning." The purpose of evaluation is to facilitate learning and to help the various audiences understand what learning is occuring.

Assessment Overview for Writing

What	How	Who	When	Documentation
Concepts about Literacy/Attitudes to Writing	• Parent Survey Sheet: expectations, strengths, weaknesses	Parents	Week 1; new entrants	Parent Survey Sheet
	• Student Survey Sheet: interests, strengths, weaknesses	Student	Week 1; new entrants	Student Survey Sheet
	• Student Self-Evaluation Form	Student	2 or 3 times a year	Proforma: Am I becoming a Good Writer?
	• Observations	Teacher	Continuous	Observation book or individual student cards; checklists
	• Informal parent contact	Teacher/ parent	As required	As above
Prewriting Strategies •considering possibilities for topic, genre, purpose •exploring (collecting and connecting) •making plans and rehearsing	• Personal Topic Lists	Student	Continuous; regular review	"Things I Might Write About" (written inside writing folder)
	• Prewriting discussion	Teacher/ small group	Continuous	Chart of focus questions
	• Observations	Teacher	Continuous	Observation book or individual cards; checklists
	• Modeled writing	Teacher/ Students	At least weekly	Lesson notes or work plan

Assessment Overview for Writing *continued*

Category	Method	Who	Frequency	Proforma / Resources
Writing Strategies •strategies for drafting and revising •strategies for handling mechanics	• Student Self-Evaluation Form	Student	2 or 3 times a year	Proforma: Am I becoming a Good Writer?
	• Observations	Teacher	Continuous	Observation book or individual cards; checklists
	• Writing conferences	Teacher/individuals or small groups	Continuous; as required	As above
	• Teaching groups	As above	Continuous; as required	As above
	• Study of have-a-go cards	Teacher	Periodically	Checklists
Post-Writing Strategies •making decisions about continuing •preparing for publishing •presenting to an audience and reflecting on responses	• Student Self-Evaluation Form	Student	2 or 3 times a year	Proforma: Am I becoming a Good Writer?
	• Observations	Teacher	Continuous	Observation book or individual cards; checklists
	• Writing conferences	Teacher/individuals of small groups	Continuous; as required	As above
	• Teaching groups	As above	Continuous; as required	As above
	• Editing guidelines	Student	As relevant	Editing checklist
Aspects of Written Products •meaning (ideas, focus, field) •organization (genre, form) •language (grammar, usage, sentence structure, vocabulary, style, mood, voice) •spelling •mechanics (handwriting, punctuation, layout)	Student Self-Evaluation Form	Student	2 or 3 times a year	Proforma: Am I becoming a Good Writer?
	• Global writing assessment (final product sample)	Teacher	At least twice a year (more often when teacher is unsure of particular student's development)	Proforma: Writing Assessment
	• Writing folder	Teacher/students	Periodically	Observation book or individual cards; checklists
	• Journal	Teacher/students	Periodically	As above

Adapted from AWRITE Project Team (1991) South Australian Dept. of Educ.

Chapter 7

Keeping Parents Informed

M ost parents want their children to be effective readers and writers. Because many parents equate reading and writing with phonics and spelling, they need, and have the right, to feel adequately informed about their children's skills in these areas.

Parents are children's first language teachers. They are remarkably effective in teaching children to talk—and their interest and responsibility for language doesn't stop there. Most parents continue to observe and monitor their children's written language development as they enter school. They want their children to learn to read and write. Since most of today's parents were educated in schools that provided direct instruction for spelling and phonics, it's no surprise that they believe that their children should be taught the same way. What's a whole language teacher to do? Communication is the key.

Informing Parents

Show parents how you teach phonics and spelling while still focusing on meaning. For example, you could say, "Of course, I teach phonics and spelling in many ways throughout the day. Let me show you." Following are a few workable strategies for doing just that.

Information Sessions

Before parents form misconceptions about your whole language teaching, organize a parent information session to explain that you do teach phonics and spelling, but you do so in the context of real writing and reading. You may find it particularly helpful to actually demonstrate a few skills lessons that directly involve parents in the activities. Be sure to leave time for questions and end by inviting the parents to visit your classroom on a regular basis.

You also could use an Authors' Night as a way to gather parents together so that you can explain how you are emphasizing *more* than phonics and spelling in your students' reading-writing program. To demonstrate your students' successes, for example, have them read aloud some of the pieces they have written, display other pieces of their writing throughout the room, and point out what children know and what they are learning.

Another useful format is a workshop that lets parents experience learning phonics and spelling through both traditional and whole language methods. In such a workshop, they will be able to compare the two methods and decide which is more effective for learning graphophonic connections.

Parents can experience the difficulty of learning to read with the following workshop devised by Elaine Vilscek. She uses Christina Rosetti's poem "Who Has Seen the Wind?" and the "new" alphabet (see pages 153-155 in the Appendix).

Parent Workshop

1. After you introduce the "new" alphabet and review the sounds, make up a few examples for practicing the sounds. Plan this activity as a simulation of traditional phonics instruction.

2. Introduce the words from the first two lines of the poem on flash cards. Make this a simulation of traditional sight word instruction.

3. After you present the poem "Who Has Seen the Wind?"—written in the "new" alphabet—ask for volunteers to read it aloud.

4. After you read the poem again to the parents, ask them to join in on the reading as you point to the words. Then repeat the reading to be certain that most have the meaning and the rhythm of the poem. (Some will have memorized the words of the poem by this point.) Finally, ask the parents to read the poem independently then in unison. Afterwards, as you point to the word *wind*, ask, "Does anyone know what this word is? Can you find the word again in the poem?" This activity should be a simulation of the shared book experience.

5. Afterwards, discuss which way to learn to read seemed less threatening by asking, "Which way were you better able to focus on meaning?"

Newsletters

Weekly newsletters are great vehicles for informing parents of upcoming topics and themes, enlisting their help for send-home activities, and explaining new strategies their children have learned and will be practicing at home. Teachers thank parent volunteers publicly in the newletters to encourage more volunteers. Another strategy that some teachers of older children use is to have their students actually write all or a portion of the newsletter every week.

Open-Door Policy

There are many ways that you can make parents feel welcome in your classroom. For starters, you can hang a welcome sign on your classroom door. Some teachers also go one step further by placing their professional reading library on a shelf by the door. On a sign over the shelf, they invite parents to check out the books so that they can learn more about the theory behind the language program the teacher uses. Still other teachers write up brief classroom guidebooks to help parents and other visitors better understand their classroom activities and routines. In some classrooms, children provide visitors with guided tours of the learning areas and activities.

When parents come into your classroom, be sure that their children always show them their writing folders and personal spelling lists, their literature logs, and their reading and writing activities. If feasible, also encourage the parents to join in on any activities in progress. Finally, display your students' works all over the room so that the signs of their progress will be easily evident.

Parent Helpers

Any parents who volunteer to help in your classroom will get to see firsthand how you teach spelling and phonics. At the same time, they can be a big help to you. To reward them for their efforts, give them meaningful tasks that get them working directly with the children. In that way, they will experience the same kind of satisfaction and appreciation that you do. When parents feel welcome and spend time in their children's classroom, they gain a better understanding of your curriculum and develop trust in you as a professional.

Reporting to Parents

There is growing evidence that the more parents, teachers, and children are actively involved together in teaching and learning processes, the more successful schools are in educating children. Most parents want to be well-informed about their children's progress and appreciate any opportunity to share in their children's evaluation. However, for those parents who never come to school voluntarily, an effective reporting system can make them feel more a part of their children's education.

Conferences

When you invite parents to a conference, ask them to bring in evidence of their child's growth in reading and writing that was done at home. Such a task will make a conference one in which everyone is actively participating. In the same team spirit, you might want to invite your students to participate in or even to preside over the next conference with their parents.

Whole language teachers who assess students, as suggested in Chapter 6, will always have considerable artifacts that provide evidence of what their students know and are learning about phonics and spelling. These teachers usually ask parents to come early and spend some time prior to the conference examining their child's portfolio with their child, listening to an audiotape of their child reading, and/or watching a brief videotape of their child reading and writing. Other teachers send these materials home and ask parents to write their own evaluation in collaboration with their child. This evaluation then becomes a part of the conference itself. Because these types of conferences are interactive, they promote the shared responsibility for learning.

Report Cards

Many teachers feel that most existing report cards don't adequately report what their students really know. For instance, the third-grade teachers at Coal Creek Elementary School in Boulder, Colorado, were dissatisfied with their district report card because it didn't reflect their whole language curriculum. As a result, they sought and received administrative support to pilot a new reporting form that could be adapted for the whole school.

After they developed a draft report form that better explained the intended outcomes of their curriculum, they interviewed parents to find out which parts of the form were confusing, misleading, or contained unnecessary information. They also asked parents what else they wanted to know about their children's learning progress. From those extremely valuable interviews, the teachers revised their report form. Below and on page 140 there is a double page from a sample report card that may help you get started with a different approach to the reporting of your students' progress. As you look it over, keep in mind the great results that you can achieve if you get the support of your administration and if you work closely with parents.

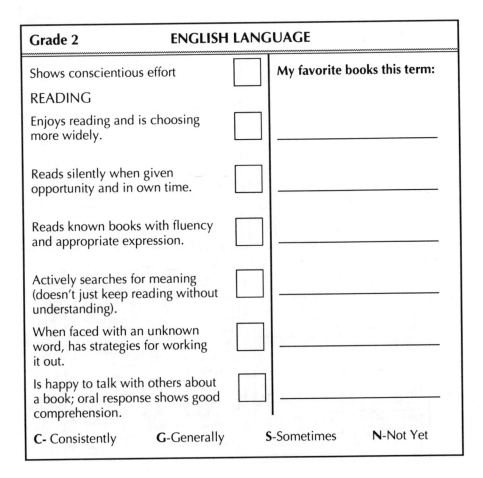

Grade 2	ENGLISH LANGUAGE	
Shows conscientious effort	☐	**My favorite books this term:**
READING		
Enjoys reading and is choosing more widely.	☐	_____
Reads silently when given opportunity and in own time.	☐	_____
Reads known books with fluency and appropriate expression.	☐	_____
Actively searches for meaning (doesn't just keep reading without understanding).	☐	_____
When faced with an unknown word, has strategies for working it out.	☐	_____
Is happy to talk with others about a book; oral response shows good comprehension.	☐	_____
C- Consistently **G-**Generally	**S-**Sometimes **N-**Not Yet	

Grade 2   **ENGLISH LANGUAGE**

WRITING

Enjoys writing. ☐

Writing has a sequence of connected ideas. ☐

Rereads writing and is happy to make changes when dissatisfied. ☐

Happy to discuss writing and to receive feedback. ☐

Writes complete, meaningful sentences. ☐

Writes in different forms for different purposes. ☐

SPELLING

Confidently attempts spelling. ☐

Temporary spellings are logical and readable. ☐

Knowledge of sound/symbol correspondences growing. ☐

Uses dictionary confidently. ☐

Can spell a core of common words. ☐

Puts effort into learning personal spelling. ☐

My favorite pieces I've written this term:

_____

_____

_____

_____

_____

_____

_____

_____

_____

Answering Questions Parents Commonly Ask

Whenever parents ask questions, you can be assured that they are interested and concerned about their children's education, and interest is the first step toward help and cooperation. First, however, you must give them satisfying answers to questions—such as the following—that are frequently asked about the teaching of phonics and spelling in a whole language classroom.

1. **Do you teach phonics and spelling in a whole language classroom?** Yes! Phonics and spelling are based on the graphophonic cues in the English language. Everyone communicates by using these graphophonic cues simultaneously with meaning and grammar cues, but in a whole language classroom, teachers don't teach letter/sound correspondences according to the traditional "sound of the week" schedule. They also don't teach a list of spelling words in a workbook that are unrelated to anything else their students are working on. Instead, their phonics and spelling instruction is driven by the texts the children are reading and by what the children's writing reveals about their knowledge of spelling patterns.

2. **How do you teach phonics and spelling without workbooks?** Teachers teach phonics and spelling both through inquiry and through direct instruction, according to their students' needs. As children read quality literature, they need to know particular phonic connections, and as they write for real purposes and for real audiences, they also need to know particular spelling patterns. Therefore, phonics and spelling are taught within the context of reading and writing authentic texts. (You may want to refer your parents to the *Possum Magic* example in Chapter 3 on pages 44-48.)

3. **What's the best way for me to help my child when he comes to an unknown word?** First, pause and provide time for him to figure it out for himself. If your child is not confident with decoding, supply the word rather than asking him to "sound it out." As your child gains confidence, pose questions such as, "What

word would make sense there?" or "What would happen if you skipped the word and kept reading? Do you think you could figure it out then?" When you interrupt the meaning that is being formed between reader and author by asking your child to focus on letter/sounds, you are teaching him inadvertently that reading is saying the words correctly. This is not the message you want to convey. Instead, the message should be that reading is for meaning.

4. **What should I say when my child asks me how to spell a word?** Respond first by saying, "How do you think you spell it?" or "How would you spell it if you didn't have anyone to help you?" When very young children begin showing an interest in writing, they usually ask their parents to write for her. As they learn what the letters are and how to form them, they usually ask how words are spelled. At that point, you should spell the word for her. However, once children have made phonetic connections, they can make fairly accurate attempts at spelling themselves, even if at this point they are only representing words with a single letter or just consonants.

As a parent, you need to praise these early attempts and encourage more writing. If your child insists you spell words for her, ask her to help you, but keep trying to shift the spelling attempts back to her. For example, instead of telling your child that you can't read her writing, ask her to read it to you. Then praise any letter/sound connection she makes. If there doesn't seem to be any connections, don't worry—some children need a little extra time to make these connections. You may, however, want to have your child's hearing checked—just to make sure there is not a problem in that area that you just haven't detected.

When you read to your child, you also may want to occasionally point out connections between letters and sounds. You could play with magnetic letters on the refrigerator door or even write words and point out beginning sounds. You also could take dictation for your child. Then as she starts to hear beginning sounds, play games that help her listen for the middle and ending sounds in words. Eventually connections will be made—be patient!

5. **What's wrong with spellings lists?** Believe it or not, most of the words you learned how to spell in school were not learned from lists! (Not even 20 words a week could account for all of the words you know.) Effective spelling programs, however, often use spelling lists that are generated through the reading-writing program as *one* component. Spelling programs of whole language teachers go far beyond word lists.

6. **Don't invented spellings teach children to spell incorrectly?** Learning to spell is much like learning to talk. When children learn to talk, parents celebrate all their babblings that sound like *mama* and *dada*. Invented, or temporary, spelling is very similar to those first "words." In the same way, you need to celebrate children's first attempts at writing words. Initially, very young children are not able to write entire words. In fact, when they begin attending to letter/sound connections, they often begin writing words using only the initial consonant or the predominant sound of the word. Because spelling is a developmental process, children need praise for what they can do. With lots of modeling and encouragement, children will learn more phonics and spelling patterns that will help them move toward more conventional spellings.

7. **Why aren't all the words on my child's papers spelled correctly?** When children are composing rough drafts, they may use dashes in place of letters they don't know, or they may underline words they're not sure they've spelled correctly. Many teachers don't encourage them to go back and correct all the words they don't know—particularly if they are only writing drafts that won't be published. When writing is to "go public," however, teachers usually expect their students to attend to spelling and they may even ask students to correct a certain number of words, depending on their abilities. Some teachers also ask parent helpers or a rotating editorial committee of children to help in correcting all remaining misspelled words before a piece is published.

Because spelling is a developmental process, not every child is capable of giving the same amount of attention to spelling. The more children write for real purposes and real audiences, however, the more motivated they will be to attend to their spelling and the easier it will become for them. When teachers overburden their student writers with spelling, the children often turn off to writing and have no motivation to spell at all.

When your child brings home papers with misspelled words, first discuss the purpose of his piece of writing. Ask him if he can find a word that they would like to work on, and be sure to praise him for finding a misspelled word! If the word has a missing letter, ask where the letter would go and what he thinks the letter is. Again offer praise for knowing where the letter is missing—even if he doesn't know the missing letter. Chances are that the missing letter is a vowel and that your child will likely even be able to supply a vowel (though it may not be the correct one). Strategies like this are a big step toward learning to spell.

8. **What can I do at home to help my child with phonics and spelling?** Read as much as you can to your child—every day! When she wants to read along with you, encourage her and give her just the words she doesn't know. When you come to a section of the text that you think she might know, stop and wait with expectation—because children love to join in if they can. Celebrate when she reads with some success. You might ask such questions as "How did you know it was that word?" or "How did you figure that out?"

Also, let your child see you write for many purposes—such as grocery lists, phone messages, and letters. When you come to words you're unsure of, comment on that. Let her know it's normal to be unsure of spelling sometimes. Then ask her to add to your shopping lists, write letters to family and friends, make cards, and take phone messages. As she works, encourage her to figure out the spellings before you provide them, and then congratulate her for the parts of the words she gets right.

Another helpful strategy is to help your child become word watchers by playing word games—some of which are suggested at the end of Chapter 3. You also could play commercially available word games with her—such as Spellbound™, Scrabble™, Boggle!™, and Junior Trivial Pursuit™.

APPENDIX

Phonic Elements for Sound Charts

The most common spelling patterns of vowel sounds in English are provided on the next four pages. The International Phonetic Alphabet symbols are also included for your reference. The lists will assist you in making Sound Charts such as the one below (see page 48 in Chapter 3). Include boxes for all common spellings of the sound and leave at least one blank space for dialect differences or other spelling patterns.

The Phonic Elements can also serve as a checklist to record when you have emphasized particular sounds in your teaching. The lists and Sound Charts may also assist you in evaluation of spelling patterns.

ō	rope	
o	**ow**	**ew**
both comb go open so no smoke note rose broken folk o'clock almost over	sow tow show row know crow blown own yellow grown shown	sew
o-e home nose gone cone chrome alone cyclone Rome cope rope tone slope bone those smoke joke aerodrome spoke phone gnome	below meadow fellow	**ough** dough
	oa boat road toad groan coat oatmeal floated oak cocoa foam moan	**oe** toe poem goes Joe hoe
		oo
		oh
		au

148

Consonant Sounds

Sound	I.P.A. Symbol	Possible spellings	Comments
/b/	b	b-bat bb-hobby	
/c/ or /k/	k	c-cat ch-chorus cc-account k-kick ck-black qu-bouquet	
/d/	d	d-dog ed-rolled dd-ladder	
/f/	f	f-fish ff-coffee ph-phone gh-laugh	
/g/	g	g-goat gg-egg gh-ghost gu-guard	
/h/	h	h-he wh-who	
/j/	dʒ	j-jam g-giant dge-judge d-soldier	
/l/	l	l-lid ll-ball	
/m/	m	m-mud mm-summer mb-climb	
/n/	n	n-nut kn-knot nn-inn gn-gnome	
/p/	p	p-pot pp-pepper	
/r/	r	r-rat rr-terror wr-write rh-rhyme	
/s/	s	s-see sc-scent ss-moss c-cent	

Sound	I.P.A. Symbol	Possible Spellings	Comments
/t/	t	t-top ed-jumped pt-receipt tt-little bt-debt	
/v/	v	v-vat f-of	
/w/	w	w-water	
/y/	j	y-yet i-onion Note also /y-oo/ as in beauty, few	
/z/	z	z-zebra zz-jazz ss-scissors s-is	
/sh/ voiceless	ʃ	sh-ship s-sugar ss-tissue ci-special ch-machine ce-ocean sci-conscience sch-schnauzer ti-nation	
/sh/ voiced	ʒ	s-treasure si-fusion z-azure	
/ch/	tʃ	ch-chicken ch-catch te-righteous c-cello ti-question	
/ng/	ŋ	ng-sing n-sink	
/th/ voiceless	θ	th-thin	
/th/ voiced	ð	th-then	

Vowels and Diphthongs (glides)

Sound	I.P.A. Symbol	Possible Spellings	Comments
/c<u>a</u>t/	æ	a-cat ai-plait	
/p<u>e</u>t/	e	e-egg ei-heifer a-any eo-leopard ai-said	
/p<u>i</u>g/	ï	i-ink ie-sieve ui-build a-village o-women u-busy y-symbol	
/p<u>o</u>t/	o	o-hot a-watch au-auction ou-cough*	
/p<u>u</u>p/	ʌ	u-under o-some oo-blood ou-trouble a-garage	
/c<u>a</u>ke/	eɪ	a-baby a (e)-cake† ai-rain ay-hay ea-break et-ballet ey-they	
/f<u>ee</u>t/	i:	e-equal e (e)-these† ee-seed ea-tea ei-receive ey-key eo-people i-ski ie-field	
/b<u>i</u>ke/	ai	i-child i (e)-nice† ie-pie ig-sign igh-night ai-aisle ei-height ey-eye uy-buy y-fly	
/t<u>o</u>e/	əʊ	o-both o (e)-bone† oa-boat oe-toe oo-brooch ow-snow ough-though ew-sew eau-beau	
/r<u>u</u>le/ **Note:** This is the 'oo' sound (not 'yoo')	u:	u-ruby u (e)-rude† ui-fruit ew-grew o-move oo-pool ou-troupe ough-through	

The NAME of the letter 'u' is "yoo"; the SOUND is "oo" (as in 'June,' 'Susan,' etc.) In some words, the sound /y/ is pronounced before the /oo/, which accounts for the confusion. This varies with dialect. The word 'tune' is sometimes pronounced /t-oo-n/ and sometimes /t-yoo-n/.

Sound	I.P.A. Symbol	Possible Spellings	Comments
/c<u>a</u>r/	ɑː	a-father al-palm ar-car au-laugh* e-sergeant ear-heart	
/f<u>er</u>n/	ɜː	er-term ear-learn ir-bird or-word ur-fur our-journey	
/p<u>or</u>t/	ɔ	o-morning oa-broad ou-fought a-tall al-talk aw-saw	
/b<u>oo</u>k/	ʊ	u-pull o-wolf oo-look ou-could	
/h<u>ow</u>/	ɑʊ	ou-shout ough-bough ow-brown	
/b<u>oy</u>/	ɔɪ	oi-boil oy-toy	
/h<u>air</u>/	eə	air-chair are-dare ere-there eir-their ear-pear	
/h<u>ear</u>/	ɪə	ear-beard eer-deer ere-here ier-fierce	
/t<u>ou</u>r/	ʊ	our-tour	

Notes:

* differences in dialect or pronunciation will result in different classifications.

† In these spellings, the first vowel on its own stands for the identified sound; a "final e" is *not* required to make the vowel "say" anything at all (even though this has been the traditional explanation to children). For example, in the word 'rake,' the letter 'a' represents the sound (ei).

Letters of the New Alphabet

+ -A	apple	
∞ -B	book	
-C	cat	
-D	dog	
⊗ -E	egg	
▽ -F	fan	
-G	gift	
-H	hat	
∨ -I	ink	
☆ -J	jelly	
-K	kiss	
< -L	lock	
-M	mouth	
-N	nose	
-O	oak	
× -P	pot	
✳ -Q	question	
⌐ -R	rug	
⊥ -S	shoe	
∧ -T	tepee	
-U	umbrella	
⊕ -V	vine	
-W	wart	
⋈ -X	xylophone	
⊃ -Y	yoyo	
-Z	zebra	

Who Has Seen the Wind?

Who has seen the wind?
  Neither I nor you,
But when the leaves hang trembling,
  The wind is passing through.

Who has seen the wind?
  Neither you nor I,
But when the trees bow down their heads,
  The wind is passing by.

by Christina Rosetti

Checkpoints for Emergent Readers

Skills/strategies	Checkpoint			
	1 not apparent yet	2 sometimes	3 generally	4 consistently
Requests books and other print to be read				
Turns pages and understands orientation of book				
Chooses to look at books				
"Reads" familiar books to self (or others), providing accurate renditions				
"Reads" environmental print				
Predicts next word in text when adult reader pauses (especially in predictable or familiar text)				
Recites whole phrases from favorite stories (outside of story-reading context)				
Retells past experiences and/or stories heard				
Points to print when asked, "Where does it say that?"				
"Reads" along when being read to				
Points to individual words while being read to				
Identifies and names most letters				
Is beginning to notice the letters and sounds at the beginning and end of words				
Attempts to create his or her own meaningful text through scribbles, letter-like symbols, letters, or words predominantly spelled with consonants				

Developed by D. Powell in conjunction with McClanahan & Co.

Checkpoints for Novice Readers

Skills/strategies	Checkpoint			
	1 not apparent yet	2 sometimes	3 generally	4 consistently
Appreciates silent reading opportunities				
Shows a one-to-one match between speech and print when reading				
Understands the concept of words				
"Reads" a book confidently after hearing the text once				
Uses syntax, semantics and graphophonics for decoding unknown words				
Makes meaningful substitutions				
Self-corrects nonmeaningful substitutions				
Predicts next word or idea				
Uses picture cues for decoding				
Comprehends what he or she has read and produces an accurate retelling				
Recognizes common sight words				
Recognizes most consonants				
Recognizes common spellings of vowel sounds				
Reads some texts independently but still needs limited support from an independent reader				
Creates own text using temporary spelling and some conventional spelling				

Developed by D. Powell in conjunction with McClanahan & Co.

Checkpoints for Independent Readers

Skills/strategies	Checkpoint			
	1 not apparent yet	2 sonetimes	3 generally	4 consistently
Takes risks in reading new materials				
Self-corrects through rereading to make sense				
Reads silently (younger children may subvocalize)				
Makes predictions about words using three cue systems interdependently				
Applies appropriate comprehension strategies to construct meaning				
Examines and extends meaning after reading				
Varies reading strategies for purpose in reading				
Selects a range of genre and is familiar with these purposes				
Uses conventional spelling somewhat consistently				
Reading broader range of genre influences personal writing				

Developed by D. Powell in conjunction with McClanahan & Co.

Checkpoints for Emergent Spellers

Skills/strategies	Checkpoint			
	1 not apparent yet	2 sometimes	3 generally	4 consistently
Spelling in the Writing Context Wants to write Has a have-a-go spirit; willing to invent temporary spellings Displays an interest in words Experiments with words/letters				
Visual Knowledge Can write own name Can write a few common words from memory Uses some common visual patterns (such as -ing) Attends to visual features of words (such as double letters)				
Knowledge of Alphabet Knows letter names Writes some letters Distinguishes between letters and numerals Distinguishes between upper- and lowercase				
Sound Symbol Repationship Uses initial consonant or dominant consonant to represent words (I M S = I am six) Uses consonants to represent dominant sounds (sd = slide) Uses consonants or vowels for each dominant sound (apl = apple; wet = went) Uses letter names to represent sounds (AT = eighty; U = you) Bases spelling on own articulation				
Concepts about Print Uses spaces (or space markers) between words Understands left-to-right directionality Understands top-to-bottom directionality				

Checkpoints for Novice Spellers

Skills/strategies	Checkpoint			
	1 not apparent yet	2 sometimes	3 generally	4 consistently
Spelling in the Writing Context Interested in and uses new words Growing in confidence and uses own resources Spells more words automatically Uses temporary spellings confidently				
Visual Knowledge Recognizes many conventional spellings Aware of some irregular spellings Aware of more complex visual patterns (*ion, ough*) Interested in word features				

Sound-Symbol Relationships
More aware of visual patterns and
  common morphemic units
Writes letters for every sound unit (*bakr =
  baker; chruk = truck*)
Uses a vowel or vowel combination in
  each syllable (*jirarf-giraffe; elufunt =
  elephant*)
Vowel digraphs appearing more often
  (*peepl = people; baik = bake*)				

Morphemic Knowledge
Understands compound words (*foot + ball
  = football*)
Uses common prefixes and suffixes (*un-,
  -er,-ly*)
Uses common inflectional endings (*-ing,
  -ed, -es*)
Recognizes base words (*apart*)				

Stategies for Self Support Uses environmental print Uses resources such as junior dictionaries Seeks assistance and response from others Uses proofreading techniques Knows some ways to learn words Can spell 100 most common words automatically				

Checkpoints for Independent Spellers

Skills/strategies	Checkpoint			
	1 not apparent yet	2 sometimes	3 generally	4 consistently
Spelling in the Writing Context Uses interesting and unusual words Uses experience and knowledge of the 　written language to "word solve" Attempts correct spelling in writing Spells most words automatically				
Visual Knowledge Recognizes and corrects misspelled words Recognizes conventional spellings Knowledge of silent letters (*gnome, align*) Correctly uses words with irregular 　spellings				
Sound Symbol Relationships Aware of more common spelling patterns 　for a sound (oa for /o/) Aware of various spellings for the vowel 　sounds Uses homophones correctly (*bored, board*)				
Morphemic Knowledge Shows interest in word structures and 　derivations Developing knowledge of Greek and Latin 　roots (*dico* - "to say;" *ject* -"to throw") Developing awareness of more difficult 　prefixes and suffixes (*pro*ject, project*ile*) Understands sounds may change from 　roots to deriviations (sign-signature) Can correct words by referring to related 　words (major/majority; meant/mean)				
Strategies for Self-Support Has a critical attitude towards spelling Uses mnemonics to help memory Uses dictionary, thesaurus, and other print 　resources Uses proofreading strategies efficiently Can spell 250 most common words Has a clear, fluent, handwriting style				

References

Adams, M. (1990). *Beginning to Read: Thinking and Learning about Print.* Cambridge, MA.: The MIT Press.

Ashton-Warner, S. (1963). *Teacher.* Simon and Schuster, Inc.

Atwell, N. (1987a). *In the Middle.* Portsmouth, NH: Heinemann.

Barmby, S. & Jones, K. (1991). *Assisting Learners: A Holistic Approach to Literacy Improvement.* Melbourne: Ringwood School Support Centre.

Base, G. (1986). *Animalia* New York: Harry N. Abrams, Inc.

Bean, W. & Bouffler, C. (1987). *Spell by Writing.* Portsmouth, NH: Heinemann.

Britton, J. et.al. (1975). *The Development of Writing Abilities, 11-18.* London: Macmillan Education.

Brown, H. and Mathie, V. (1990). *Inside Whole Language.* Portsmonth, NH. Heinemann

Burke, C. (1980). "Reading Inventory" in Farr, B. & Strickler, D. (Eds.) *Reading Comprehension: An instructional videotape series resource guide.* Bloomington, IN: Indiana University Language Education.

Calkins, L. (1986). *The Art of Teaching Writing.* Portsmouth, NH: Heinemann.

Calkins, L. (1983). *Lessons from a Child.* Portsmouth, NH: Heinemann.

Clay, M. (1991). *Becoming Literate: The Construction of Inner Control.* Portsmouth, NH: Heinemann.

Clay, M. (1979). *Reading: The Patterning of Complex Behavior.* Portsmouth, NH: Heinemann.

Cowley, J. & Melser, J. (1980). *Hairy Bear.* Auckland, NZ: Shortland Publication.

Dunn, S. (1987). *Butterscotch Dreams: Chants for Fun and Learning.* Portsmouth, NH: Heinemann.

Dunn., S. (1990). *Crackers & Crumbs: Chants for Whole Language.* Portsmouth, NH: Heinemann.

Fisher, Bobbi. (1991). *Joyful Learning: A Whole Language Kindergarten.* Portsmouth, NH: Heinemann.

Fulwiler, T. (1987). "Building a Dining Room Table: Dialogue Journal about Reading," in Fulwiler, T. *The Journal Book.* Portsmouth, NH: Boynton Cook.

Fulwiler, T. (1987). *The Journal Book.* Portsmouth, NH: Boynton Cook.

163

Fox, Mem. (1983). *Possum Magic.* Harcourt Brace Jovanovich.

Gentry, J.R. (November, 1982). "An Analysis of Developmental Spelling in GYNS AT WRK" in *Reading Teacher,* 192-200.

Gentry, J.R. & Gillet, J.W. (1993). *Teaching Kids to Spell.* Portsmouth, NH: Heinemann.

Goodman, Y. (1980). "Kid Watching: an Alternative to Testing," in Farr, B. & Strickler, D. (Eds.) *Reading Comprehension: An Instructional Videotape Series Resource Guide.* Bloomington, IN: Indiana University Language Education.

Goodman, Y., Watson, D. & Burke, C. (1989). *Reading Miscue Inventory: Alternative Procedures.* Katonah, NY: Richard C. Owen.

Goswami, U. & Bryant, P. (1990). *Phonological Skills and Learning to Read.* East Sussex, U.K.: Lawrence Erlbaum Associates, Ltd.

Graves. D. (1984). *A Researcher Learns to Write: Selected Articles and Monographs.* Portsmouth, NH: Heinemann.

Graves, D. (1983). *Writing: Teachers and Children at Work.* Portsmouth, NH: Heinemann.

Hall, M.A. (1976, 2nd edition). *Teaching Reading as a Language Experience.* Columbus, OH: Charles E. Merrill Publishing Company.

Hansen, J. (1987). *When Writers Read.* Portsmouth, NH: Heinemann.

Harris, T. & Hodges, R. (1981). *A Dictionary of Reading and Related Terms.* Newark, DE: International Reading Association.

Harste, J., Woodward, V. & Burke, C. (1984). *Language Stories and Literacy Lessons.* Portsmouth, NH: Heinemann.

Henderson, E. & Beers, J.W. (Eds.) (1980). *Developmental and Congative Aspects of Learning to Spell: A Reflection of Word Knowledge.* Newark, DE: International Reading Association.

Holdaway, D. (1979). *Foundations of Literacy.* Portsmouth, NH: Heinemann.

Holdaway, D. (1980). *Independence in Reading.* Portsmouth, NH: Heinemann.

Holdaway, D. (1984). *Stability and Change in Literacy Learning.* Portsmouth, NH: Heinemann.

Hornsby, D. & Parry, J. (1992). *Language and Integrated Learning* in Pidgon & Woolley (eds.), The Big Picture. Melbourne: Eleanor Curtin Publishing.

Hornsby, D., Sukarna, D. & Parry, J. (1988). *Read On: A Conference Approach to Reading.* Portsmouth, NH: Heinemann.

Hornsby, D. Parry, J. & Sukarna, D. (1993). *Teach On: Strategies for a Whole Language Classroom.*Portsmouth, NH: Heinemann.

Magorian, M. (1983). *Goodnight, Mr. Tom.* Middlesex, London: Penguin.

Martin, B. Jr. (1967). *Brown Bear, Brown Bear, What Do You See?* New York: Holt, Rinehart & Winston.

Meek, M. (1981). *Learning to Read.* London: The Bodley Head.

Melser, J. & Cowley, J. (selectors) (1980). *In a Dark, Dark Wood.* Auckland, NZ: Shortland Publication.

Pappas, C. et. al. (1990). *An Integrated Language Perspective in the Elementary School.* White Plains, NY: Longman.

Parry, J. & Hornsby, D. (1988). *Write On: A Conference Approach to Writing.* Portsmouth, NH: Heinemann.

Paulsen, G. (1987). *Hatchet.* New York: Puffin Books.

Peters, M. (1975). *Diagnostic and Remedial Spelling Manual.* London: Macmillian.

Pigdon, K. & Woolley, M. (1992). *The Big Picture.* Melbourne: Eleanor Curtin Publishing.

Powell, D. & Butler, A. (ed) (1989). *Poems in Your Pocket.* Crystal Lake, IL: Rigby.

Powell, D. & Butler, A. (ed) (1989). *Splishes and Sploshes.* Crystal Lake, IL: Rigby.

Powell, D. (1989). *Checkpoints for Reading* (copy). New York: McClanahan & Co.

Powell, D. (1990). *Learning Graphophonics in Whole Language Classrooms.* Crystal Lake,. IL: Rigby.

Pulvertaft, Ann. (1978). *Carry on Reading.* Ashton Scholastic.

Rawls, W. (1976). *Summer of the Monkeys.* New York: Dell.

Rosenblatt, L. (1978). *The Reader, the Text, the Poem: The Transactional Theory of the Literary Work.* Carbondale, IL: Southern Illinois University Press.

Routman, R. (1991). *Invitations: Changing as Teachers and Learners K-12.* Portsmouth, NH: Heinemann.

Smith, F. (1982). *Understanding Reading.* New York: Holt, Rinehart and Winston.

Staton, J. (1987). "The Power of Responding in Dialogue Journals," in Fulwiler, T. *The Journal Book.* Portsmouth, NH: Boynton Cook.

Van Allen, R. (1976). *Language Experiences in Communication.* Boston, MA: Houghton Mifflin Company.

Weaver, C. (1988). *Reading Process and Practice: From Socio-Psycholinguistics to Whole Language.* Portsmouth, NH: Heinemann.

Weaver, C. (1990). *Understanding Whole Language: From Principles to Practice.* Portsmouth, NH: Heinemann.

White, E.B. (1952). *Charlotte's Web.* New York: HarperCollins.

A WRITE Project Team. (1991). *Literacy Assessment in Practice: R-7 Language Arts.* Adelaide, South Australia: Education Department of South Australia.

Zolotow, C. (1971). *Wake Up and Good Night.* New York: HarperCollins.

Notes

Notes